POWER XL AIR FRYER GRILL COOKBOOK

Fish and Seafood, Meat, Poultry, Pizza, Rotisserie and Dessert Recipes

By

Michael Marino

© Copyright 2021 - All rights reserved.

The content contained within this book may not be reproduced, duplicated, or transmitted without direct written permission from the author or the publisher. Under no circumstances will any blame or legal responsibility be held against the publisher, or author, for any damages, reparation, or monetary loss due to the information contained within this book, either directly or indirectly.

Legal Notice:

This book is copyright protected. It is only for personal use. You cannot amend, distribute, sell, use, quote, or paraphrase any part, or the content within this book, without the consent of the author or publisher.

Disclaimer Notice:

Please note the information contained within this document is for educational and entertainment purposes only. All effort has been executed to present accurate, up-to-date, reliable, complete information. No warranties of any kind are declared or implied. Readers acknowledge that the author is not engaged in the rendering of legal, financial, medical, or professional advice. Please consult a licensed professional before attempting any techniques outlined in this book.

By reading this document, the reader agrees that under no circumstances is the author responsible for any losses, direct or indirect, that are incurred as a result of the use of the information contained within this document, including, but not limited to: errors, omissions, or inaccuracies.

Table of Contents

INTRODUCTION 6

FISH & SEAFOOD 9

.... 11
- BACON-WRAPPED BUFFALO SHRIMP 13
- LEMON PEPPER SHRIMP 13
- MEDITERRANEAN SWORDFISH 13
- PECAN SAUCE WITH SALMON 14
- ISLAND MAHI 15
- CRISPY FISH FILLETS 15
- BEER BATTERED FISH FILLET 16
- SWORDFISH WITH HERB VINAIGRETTE 16
- MAPLE-GLAZED SALMON 17
- SMOKED SALMON 18
- FROZEN FISH FILLET 18
- PESTO SALMON 18
- SALMON WITH BROCCOLI AND CHEESE 19
- SALMON WITH SAUCE 20
- CAJUN SALMON 20
- SALMON WITH GREEN BEANS 21
- SALMON WITH COCONUT 21
- HEALTHY WHITE FISH 21
- CRAB PATTIES 22
- ISLAND SCALLOPS 22
- SUNDRIED TOMATO WITH AIR-FRIED SALMON 23
- SALMON WITH CREAMY DILL SAUCE 23
- AIR FRYER CAJUN SCALLOPS 24
- AIR FRIED SCALLOPS 24
- EASY AIR FRYER BREADED SEA SCALLOPS 25
- SHRIMP LETTUCE WRAP 25
- EGG, SHRIMP, AND AVOCADO 26
- SHRIMP, MUSHROOM, AND BROCCOLI 26
- SALMON CAKE 27
- COCONUT SHRIMP 27
- SPICY FISH FILLET 28
- CRAB CAKES 28
- BLACKENED SALMON 29
- SHRIMP POPPERS 29

MEAT RECIPES 31

- CHIPOTLE RIB EYE STEAK 35
- TERIYAKI GLAZED STEAK 35
- STEAKHOUSE RIB-EYE 36
- COUNTRY STYLE RIBS 36
- CHINESE SPARE RIB 37
- GLAZED STEAK RECIPE 37
- STEAK IN AIR FRY 38
- BBQ RIBS 38
- BEEF RIBS 39
- CUBAN PORK CHOPS 39
- SPICY LAMB CHOPS 40
- YOGURT LAMB CHOPS 40
- CLASSIC PORK CHOPS 41
- TASTY AND EASY PORK CHOPS 41
- CHINESE BBQ PORK 42
- STUFFED BEEF STEAK ROLL UP 42
- SPANISH RUB PORK BURGERS 43
- SPAGHETTI WITH MEATBALLS 43
- HAM BURGER PATTIES 44
- MEATBALLS IN TOMATO SAUCE 45
- TURKEY PANINI 45
- PORK MILANESE AND CHEESY STUFFED MUSHROOMS 46
- MOJITO LAMB RIBS 46
- SKIRT STEAK WITH BALSAMIC SHALLOTS 47
- AIR FRY LOIN LAMB CHOPS 47
- ASIAN PORK CHOPS 48
- AIR FRYER STEAK 48
- RUMP STEAK 49
- FILLED EMPANADAS 49
- SUGAR GLAZE HAM 50
- CORNED BEEF AND CABBAGE ROLLS 50
- MINTY PORK CHOPS 51
- SALT AND BLACK PEPPER STEAK 51
- MUSTARD PORK CHOPS 51
- BELL PEPPERS WITH SAUSAGES 52
- PORK CHOP WITH RASPBERRY CHIPOTLE SAUCE 52
- EASY PORK CHOPS 53
- PORK CHOPS WITH BASIL-GARLIC RUB 53
- BRINED PORK CHOPS 54
- GRILLED LAMB RECIPES 54
- STEAK STRIPS 55
- BEEF RIBS 55
- GRILLED T-BONE 55

POULTRY RECIPES 57

  59
- Cornish Hens 61
- Roasted Chicken with Herbs 61
- Fried Chicken Strips 61
- Chicken Wings 62
- Chicken Breast 62
- Chicken Tenders 63
- Buffalo wings 63
- Sweet and Spicy Chicken Wings 63
- Fried Chicken 64
- Hot and Spicy Chicken 64
- Chicken Milanese 65
- Orange Chicken 66
- Chicken Leg 66
- Easy Chicken Breasts 67
- Spicy Chicken Breast 67
- Spicy Curried Chicken Wings Recipe 68
- Chicken Wings with Sesame and soy 68
- Glazed Thighs 69
- Coconut Thai Wings 69
- Roasted Chicken with Apple 70
- Chicken Meat Patties 70
- Sesame Flavored Chicken Breast 71
- Yogurt Lime Chicken 71
- Parmesan Breaded Fried Chicken Tenders 72
- Pineapple Chicken 72
- Balsamic Vinegar Chicken Breasts 73
- Sriracha-Honey Wings 73
- Bang Chicken 74
- Chipotle Chicken Wings 74
- Ginger Chicken 75
- BBQ Wings 75
- Chicken Tomatina 75
- Maple Chicken Wing 76

ROTISSERIE RECIPES 77

  79
- Apple Maple Glazed Ham 81
- Pineapple Glazed Ham 81
- Orange Glaze Ham 81
- Sugared Glazed Ham 82
- Honey and Clove Ham 82
- Rum Glazed Ham 83
- Sweet and Spicy Glazed Ham 83
- Zesty Glazed Ham 84
- BBQ Glazed Ham 84
- Bourbon Ham 85
- Smoked Dijon Ham 85
- Cane Syrup Glazed Ham 86
- Chipotle Glazed Ham 86
- Chelsea Golden Syrup 87
- Mustard and Plum Glazed Ham 87
- Cornish Hens 87
- Buttermilk Marinated Hen 88
- Spiced Chicken 89
- Seasoned Hen 89
- BBQ Chicken 89
- Rotisserie Beef Chuck 90
- Cayenne Chicken 90
- Zesty Chicken 91
- Top Round Roast 91
- Beef Roast 92
- Marinated Beef Roast 92
- Perfect Rib Roast 93
- Aleppo Prime Rib 93
- BBQ Pork Spare Ribs 93
- Delicious Beef Back Rib 94
- Beef Back Rib 94
- Rotisserie Lamb 95
- Mediterranean Lamb 95
- MarinaTED Lamb Leg 96
- Beer Glazed Ham 96

PIZZA RECIPES 99

  101
- Supreme Pizza 103
- Chorizo Pizza 103
- Simple Air Fryer Pizza 104
- White Pizza 104
- Air Fryer Pizza 105
- Salami Pizza 105
- Pepperoni Pizza 106
- garlic Pizza 106
- Mix Vegetables Pizza 107
- Cauliflower and Spinach Pizza 108
- Veggies Pizza 108
- Artichoke Pizza 109
- Easy Mix Vegetable Pizza 109

Ultimate Veggie Pizza	110
Three Cheese Pizza	111
Sausage Pizza	111
Italian Sausage Pizza	112
Meat Lover Pizza	112
Seafood Pizza	113
Grilled Chicken Pizza	113

DESSERT RECIPES	**115**
	117
Mini Chocolate Peanut Butter Cupcakes	119
Super Moist Cupcake	119
Vanilla Cupcake	120
Fudge Brownies	120
Pignoli Cookies	121
Lemony Sweet Twists	121
Jam Filled Buttermilk Scones	122
Cinnamon Sweet Twists	122
Raisin and Oatmeal Cookies	123

Cream Puffs	123
Chocolate Filled Cream Puffs	124
Vanilla Bean Meringues	124
Lemon Meringues	125
Coconut Meringues	125
Sweet Potato Mug Cake for Two	126
Empanada Wraps	126
Mini Strawberry and Cream Pies	127
Ginger Cranberry Scones	127
Mint and Chocolate Pudding	128
Chocolate Pudding Cake	128
VANILLA CAKE	129
GRILLED PINEAPPLE	129
GRILLED BANANAS	129
GRILLED APPLE	130
CHOCLATE CHIP CUPCAKE	130

WHAT ELSE?	**131**
A MESSAGE FROM THE AUTHOR	**134**

Introduction

The power XL air fryer grill is yet another remarkable appliance that makes cooking, baking and grilling a lot more easy and tasty. The power XL air fryer grill helps you prepare some remarkable delicious food in a very easy way. It is an indoor appliance that fits easily on your kitchen counter and does magic. The power XL air fryer grill can perform 8 functions including grill, air fry, pizza, bake, and broil, sear, toast, and reheat.

It can grill a steak to air fry French fries in no time.
The power XL air fryer grill is a top-ranked appliance that has a huge capacity to cook a 10 lb chicken.

It can cook food with 70 % fewer calories from oil or fat. It is a healthy alternative to traditional deep fryers. Now you can enjoy fewer calories food items that keep you healthy with a burst of nutrition.

In this cookbook, we are covering more than 300 recipes that are listed in a wide variety of categories.

All the parts that come with the appliance are Dishwasher safe and can easily be cleaned with less or no soaking or scrubbing required.

PARTS AND ACCESSORIES

The PowerXL Air Fryer Grill comes with the following parts:

- NONSTICK GRILL PAN
- ROTISSERIE FORK
- GLASSDOOR
- PIZZA RACK
- CRISPER TRAY
- BAKING PAN
- GRILL PLATE
- DRIP TRAY WITH RECIPE BOOK

The dial functions of the air fryer XL grill allow the user to control the time and cooking function.

BUTTON AND FUNCTIONS

TEMPERATURE/DARKNESS CONTROL KNOB

It is used to set temperature ranged from 200-450 °F.

FUNCTION KNOB

The function dial is used to choose between the 8 preset functions by turning the dial.

TIME CONTROL KNOB

It is used to set the desired cooking time. Time control is available from the range of 1–120 minutes.

POWER LIGHT

Once the cooking mode and the time for cooking have been selected, the power light will turn on. Once the timer is done, the light will turn off.

CAUTION AND CLEANING TIPS

Here are some caution and cleaning tips for the appliance.

- The PowerXL Air Fryer Grill is not intended to be used by children or toddlers under the age of 8.
- It is not recommended to use an extension cord with the Grill.
- Make sure that the electric socket where the appliance is plugged into has the same voltage indicated on the Grill.
- It is not recommended to immerse the Grill in water or any other liquid.
- The grill is intended to be used indoor.
- Make sure the grill is placed on a flat, airy, and clean surface.
- The PowerXL Air Fryer grill can be cleaned easily with a damp cloth.
- It is important to clean the grill after every cooking.
- All the parts of the grill are dishwasher-safe.

Now let's begin cooking some delicious, mouthwatering, and astonishing recipes.

Fish & Seafood

Lemon Pepper Shrimp
Page 13

Pecan Sauce with Salmon
Page 14

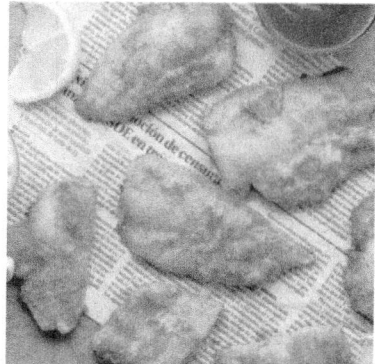
Crispy Fish Fillets
Page 15

Maple-Glazed Salmon
Page 17

Smoked Salmon
Page 18

Salmon with Green Beans
Page 21

Crab Patties
Page 22

Salmon with Creamy Dill Sauce
Page 23

Shrimp Lettuce Wrap
Page 25

BACON-WRAPPED BUFFALO SHRIMP

Prep: 10 Minutes | Cooking Time: 6 Minutes | Makes: 2 Servings

INGREDIENTS

- 20 shrimp
- 1-1/4 cup buffalo wing sauce
- 14 slices bacon
- ½ cup ranch

DIRECTIONS

1. Take a bowl and add buffalo sauce to it.
2. Then add shrimp and coat the shrimp well in the sauce.
3. Marinate the shrimp for 1 hour.
4. Now cut the bacon strips in half, wrap each half strip around the shrimp.
5. Arrange the wrapped shrimp over the grill plate.
6. Place the plate onto the middle shelf of the PowerXL Air Fryer Grill.
7. Turn the function dial to 'Grill' and set the temperature at 400°F for 6 minutes.
8. Remember to flip the shrimp halfway through.
9. Once done serve with ranch

LEMON PEPPER SHRIMP

Prep: 14 Minutes | Cooking Time: 10 Minutes | Makes: 2 Servings

INGREDIENTS

- 1 pound medium raw shrimp, peeled and deveined
- ½ cup olive oil
- 2 tablespoons lemon juice
- 1 teaspoon black pepper
- ¼ teaspoon salt

SIDE SERVINGS

- 8 ounces of pasta, cooked per directions
- 1 cup parmesan, shredded

DIRECTIONS

1. Preheat the air fryer to 450°F for 2 minutes.
2. Meanwhile, add shrimp to a large bowl and add olive oil, lemon juice, black pepper, and salt.
3. Layer parchment paper inside the crisper tray and add shrimp.
4. Add the tray to the PowerXL Air Fryer Grill.
5. Turn the function dial to 'Grill' and set the timer for 10 minutes at 400°F.
6. Once done, serve over cooked pasta using a sprinkle of cheese as a topping.

MEDITERRANEAN SWORDFISH

Prep: 15 Minutes | Cooking Time: 20 Minutes | Makes: 2 Servings

INGREDIENTS

- 2 cloves of garlic
- 2 tablespoons olive oil
- ½ tablespoon lemon juice
- 1 teaspoon cumin
- Salt, to taste
- ¼ teaspoon paprika
- Freshly ground black pepper, to taste
- ¼ teaspoon crushed red pepper
- 2 swordfish steaks, 12 ounces each
- Oil spray, for greasing

INGREDIENTS FOR SALAD

- 1 cup lettuce leaves, torn
- 1 tablespoon capers
- ½ sun-dried tomatoes
- ½ cup parsley
- ¼ black olives
- Salt, pinch
- 2 teaspoons lemon juice
- 1 teaspoon of olive oil
- ½ cup feta cheese

DIRECTIONS

1. Combine garlic, lemon juice, olive oil, and cumin, salt, paprika, black pepper, and red pepper in a bowl and coat the fish in this mixture.
2. Put the fish onto an oil-greased baking pan.
3. Put the pan on the middle shelf of the air fryer.
4. Turn the function dial to 'Grill' and set the timer to 390°F for 20 minutes.
5. Flip the fish fillet halfway through.
6. Meanwhile, mix the entire salad ingredients in a bowl.
7. Take out the fish fillet once cooking is complete, and serve the fish with the prepared salad.

PECAN SAUCE WITH SALMON

Prep: 18 Minutes | Cooking Time: 25-30 Minutes | Makes: 2 Servings

INGREDIENTS

- 2 salmon fillets, 6 ounces each
- Pinch of sea salt
- ¼ cup maple syrup
- 4 tablespoons honey

SAUCE INGREDIENTS

- 1 orange rosemary sauce
- 1/3 cup orange juice
- 2 rosemary sprigs
- 1 cup pecans, chopped
- 1 tablespoon brown sugar

Other Ingredients

- 2 tablespoons unsalted butter
- 3 tablespoons all-purpose flour

DIRECTIONS

1. Season the salmon fillets with salt and black pepper.
2. Brush the top with maple syrup.
3. Put the salmon skin-side down on an oil-greased grill plate.

4. Top with pecan and place it into the middle part of the air fryer.
5. Turn the function dial to 'Grill' and set the timer to 20 minutes at 390°F.
6. Transfer the rack to the top shelf and cook for another 2 minutes.
7. Meanwhile, prepare the sauce by mixing all of the sauce ingredients in a saucepan and simmering for 5 minutes.
8. Now mix the flour and butter in a bowl and add them to the sauce.
9. Let the sauce thicken.
10. Once done, take out the salmon and top with the prepared sauce.
11. Enjoy!

ISLAND MAHI

Prep: 10 Minutes | Cooking Time: 20 Minutes | Makes: 2 Servings

INGREDIENTS

SAUCE INGREDIENTS

- ½ cup sweetened coconut milk
- 1/3 cup soy sauce
- 2 teaspoons lemon juice
- ¼ teaspoon red pepper flakes
- ¼ teaspoon ginger

OTHER INGREDIENTS

- 3 Mahi steaks, 6 ounces each

INGREDIENTS FOR MANGO SALSA

- 2 mangoes, peeled and chopped
- ½ red bell pepper, chopped
- 1 small red onion, chopped
- 2 jalapenos, chopped
- ½ cup cilantro
- 1 tablespoon extra virgin olive oil
- 1 lime, juice only
- Salt and black pepper, to taste

DIRECTIONS

1. Take a bowl and combine all of the sauce ingredients.
2. Add the fish to the sauce and let it marinate for 30 minutes.
3. Afterwards, arrange it onto a grill plate and place it on the middle part of the air fryer.
4. Turn the function dial to the 'Grill' button and set the time to 390°F for 20 minutes.
5. Combine all of the mango salsa ingredients in a separate bowl and serve with the cooked fish.

CRISPY FISH FILLETS

Prep: 15 Minutes | Cooking Time: 20 Minutes | Makes: 2 Servings

INGREDIENTS

- 1 cup seasoned flour
- 2 eggs, organic
- ½ cup buttermilk
- 2 cups seafood fry mix
- ½ cup breadcrumbs
- 2 codfish fillets, 4-6 ounces each
- Oil spray, for greasing

DIRECTIONS

1. Whisk eggs in a bowl along with the buttermilk.
2. In a separate bowl add seafood fry mix and breadcrumbs.
3. On a baking tray, layer the flour.
4. First coat the fillets with eggs, then with flour, and at the end coat with breadcrumbs.
5. Put the fish fillet into the crisper tray lined with parchment paper, and place the tray inside the air fryer unit.
6. Turn the function dial to the 'Grill' button and set it to cook for 20 minutes at 400°F.
7. Flip the fillets halfway through the cooking process.
8. Once done, serve, and enjoy.

BEER BATTERED FISH FILLET

Prep: 18 Minutes | Cooking Time: 25 Minutes | Makes: 2 Servings

INGREDIENTS

- 1 cup all-purpose flour
- 4 tablespoons cornstarch
- 1 teaspoon baking soda
- 8 ounces buttermilk
- 2 eggs, beaten
- ½ cup all-purpose flour
- 1 teaspoon smoked paprika
- 2 tablespoons of Italian seasoning
- Salt and black pepper, to taste
- ¼ teaspoon of cayenne pepper
- 2 cod fillets, 1½-inches thick, cut into 4 pieces
- Oil spray, for greasing

DIRECTIONS

1. Combine flour, corn starch, salt, Italian seasoning, paprika, salt, pepper, and cayenne pepper and baking soda in a bowl.
2. In a separate bowl beat the egg along with the buttermilk.
3. Dip the fish into the egg mixture and then coat it with the seasoned flour.
4. Grease the fillet with oil spray.
5. Put the fillets into an air fryer baking pan lined with parchment paper.
6. Put the pan inside the air fryer.
7. Turn the function dial to 'Bake' and set the timer to 25 minutes at 390°F.
8. Once cooking is done, serve the fish.
9. Enjoy hot.

SWORDFISH WITH HERB VINAIGRETTE

Prep: 15 Minutes | Cooking Time: 20 Minutes | Makes: 3 Servings

INGREDIENTS

DRESSING INGREDIENTS

- ½ cup parsley leaves
- 1 cup basil leaves
- ½ cup mint leaves
- 2 tablespoons thyme leaves
- 1/4 teaspoon red pepper flakes

- 2 cloves of garlic
- 4 tablespoons of red wine vinegar
- ¼ cup of olive oil
- Salt, to taste

OTHER INGREDIENTS

- 1.5-pounds fish fillets, codfish
- 2 tablespoons olive oil
- Salt and black pepper, to taste
- 1 teaspoon of paprika
- 1 teasbpoon of Italian seasoning

DIRECTIONS

1. Take a food processor and dump all of the dressing ingredients in and pulse until a smooth paste is formed.
2. Transfer mixture to a bowl.
3. Season the swordfish fillet with salt, paprika, Italian seasoning, pepper, and baste it with the blended sauce.
4. Put fillets onto a foil-lined baking pan and place the pan at the bottom shelf of the air fryer.
5. Turn the function dial to 'Grill' and set it to cook for 20 minutes at 390°F.
6. Once cooked, serve the fillets with the remaining blended vinaigrette.

MAPLE-GLAZED SALMON

Prep: 15 Minutes | Cooking Time: 20 Minutes | Makes: 2 Servings

Ingredients

- ½ cup maple syrup
- 1/3 cup sweet soy sauce
- 2 tablespoons light brown sugar
- 2 ounces orange juice
- 2 tablespoons lemon juice
- ½ tablespoon red wine vinegar
- 2 teaspoons olive oil
- 2 cloves of garlic
- 1 scallion, finely chopped
- 2 salmon fillets, 4 ounces each
- Salt and ground black pepper, to taste

DIRECTIONS

1. Take a bowl and whisk the maple syrup, chopped garlic, soy sauce, brown sugar, orange juice, lemon juice, red wine vinegar, and salt.
2. Pour into a saucepan and cook until thickened.
3. Season the salmon with olive oil, salt, and black pepper.
4. Layer the air fryer basket with parchment paper.
5. Baste the salmon with the sauce and place it inside the grill plate.
6. Insert the grill plate into the unit.
7. Turn the function dial to 'Grill' and set the cooking timer for 20 minutes at 390°F.
8. Baste the fish fillets after 5 minutes of cooking and flip.
9. Once the cooking cycle has finished, brush the salmon with the sauce one last time.
10. Serve with chopped scallions.

SMOKED SALMON

Prep: 18 Minutes | Cooking Time: 20 Minutes | Makes: 4 Servings

INGREDIENTS

- 2 pounds of salmon fillets, 4 ounces each
- 6 ounces cream cheese
- 2 tablespoons mayonnaise
- 2 teaspoons of chives, fresh
- ½ teaspoon of lemon zest
- Salt and freshly ground black pepper, to taste
- 2 tablespoons of olive oil, for coating

DIRECTIONS

1. Take a bowl and combine the cream cheese, chives, mayonnaise, salt, pepper, and lemon zest.
2. Season the salmon with salt, pepper, and olive oil.
3. Put the salmon fillet onto a grill plate, and place it onto the middle position of the unit.
4. Turn the function dial to the 'Grill' button and set the timer to 20 minutes at 390°F.
5. Flip the fillets halfway through.
6. Once the salmon is ready, serve it by topping it with the mayonnaise mix.
7. Enjoy hot.

FROZEN FISH FILLET

Prep: 15 Minutes | Cooking Time: 22 Minutes | Makes: 4 Servings

Ingredients

- 4 frozen breaded fish fillets, 4 ounces each
- Oil spray, for greasing
- 1 cup mayonnaise

DIRECTIONS

1. Defrost the frozen fish fillet by taking it out of the bag.
2. Once defrosted, grease the fish fillet with oil spray on both sides.
3. Put the fish fillet onto a grill plate and place it on either the top or middle shelf.
4. Turn the function dial to the 'Grill' button and cook for 18-22 minutes at 450°F.
5. Hit the 'Start' button to start cooking.
6. Remember to flip the fillets halfway through.
7. Once cooking is done, serve the fish hot with mayonnaise.

PESTO SALMON

Prep: 15 Minutes | Cooking Time: 25 Minutes | Makes: 2 Servings

INGREDIENTS

- 2 salmon fillets, 4 ounces each
- Salt and black pepper

- 1 tablespoon of melted butter

INGREDIENTS FOR GREEN SAUCE

- 1 cup mayonnaise
- 1 teaspoon of pesto
- 6 tablespoons Greek yogurt
- Salt and black pepper, to taste

DIRECTIONS

1. First, coat the salmon with butter and season with salt and black pepper.
2. Take a serving bowl and mix mayonnaise, pesto, Greek yogurt, salt, and black pepper. Set aside.
3. Next, arrange the fish fillet on a grill plate and put it in the middle of the unit.
4. Turn the function dial to the 'Grill' button and cook the salmon for 25 minutes at 390°F.
5. Remember to flip the fish halfway through.
6. Once done, serve with the prepared pesto sauce.

SALMON WITH BROCCOLI AND CHEESE

Prep: 15 Minutes | Cooking Time: 30 Minutes | Makes: 2 Servings

INGREDIENTS

- 1 cup of broccoli
- 1/3 cup of butter, melted
- Oil spray, for greasing
- 1 cup of grated cheddar cheese
- ½ cup full-fat milk
- ½ mashed white potatoes, boiled
- ¼ teaspoon of garlic powder or garlic cloves, minced
- Salt and black pepper, to taste
- 2 fillets of salmon, 4 ounces each

DIRECTIONS

1. Season the salmon and broccoli with salt and black pepper.
2. Grease the salmon and broccoli with some oil spray.
3. Put the broccoli along with the salmon fillet into an oil-greased air grill plate.
4. Put the plate into the air fryer.
5. Turn the function dial to the 'Grill' button and set it to cook for 20 minutes at 390°F.
6. Hit Start to start the cooking.
7. After 6 minutes take out the broccoli and flip the salmon.
8. Let the cooking cycle complete.
9. Melt butter in a saucepan and add cheddar cheese and let it melt.
10. Add mashed potatoes and milk, salt, garlic powder, and black pepper.
11. Cook for a few minutes until the ingredients are combined and the sauce is creamy.
12. Serve over the cooked fish and the broccoli.
13. Enjoy.

SALMON WITH SAUCE

Prep: 15 Minutes | Cooking Time: 22 Minutes | Makes: 2 Servings

INGREDIENTS

- 2 salmon fillets, 8 ounces each
- 1 lemon cut them in half
- Salt and black pepper
- Oil spray, for greasing

SAUCE INGREDIENTS

- 1 teaspoon coriander seeds
- 1 teaspoon cumin seeds
- ½ cup pack mint leaves picked
- 1/4 small pack coriander
- 1 lemon, zest, and juice
- 2 garlic cloves
- ¼ teaspoon chilli flakes
- Salt, to taste
- 1/3 cup of water as needed

DIRECTIONS

1. First, add all of the sauce ingredients to a blender and add water.
2. Blend into a smooth sauce and set aside.
3. Season the salmon with salt, black pepper, lemon juice, and grease with oil spray.
4. Now place the salmon fillets into the air fryer grill plate.
5. Put the plate inside the unit and turn the function dial to the 'Grill' button and set the timer to 22 minutes at 390°F.
6. Flip the salmon halfway through.
7. Once the cooking is done, serve the fish fillets on a serving platter and drizzle with the sauce.
8. Enjoy.

CAJUN SALMON

Prep: 10 Minutes | Cooking Time: 18 Minutes | Makes: 2 Servings

INGREDIENTS

- 2 salmon fillets, 4 ounces each
- 1 tablespoon of Cajun seasoning
- 1 tablespoon of jerk seasoning
- 4 tablespoons of lemon, juice
- Oil spray, for greasing
- ½ cup blue cheeses dressing

DIRECTIONS

1. Mix Cajun seasoning, lemon juice, and jerk seasoning in a bowl and set aside.
2. Grease the fillet with some oil spray, and rub the spice mixture all over the fillets.
3. Now place the salmon fillets on the grill plate and put them on the middle shelf of the air fryer.
4. Turn the function dial to 'Grill', and set the temperature to 390°F for 18 minutes.
5. Remember to flip the fish halfway through.
6. Once the cooking is done, serve the fish fillets with blue cheese dressing.

SALMON WITH GREEN BEANS

Prep: 15 Minutes | Cooking Time: 15 Minutes | Makes: 2 Servings

INGREDIENTS

- 2 salmon fillets, two inches thick
- 2 teaspoons of smoked paprika
- Salt and black pepper, to taste
- 1 cup green beans
- Oil spray, for greasing

DIRECTIONS

1. Spray the salmon and green beans with some oil spray.
2. Season the salmon and green beans with smoked paprika, salt, and pepper.
3. Grease the grill plate with oil spray.
4. Put the salmon fillets on the middle shelf inside the grill plate along with the green beans on the crisper tray on the lower shelf.
5. Turn the function dial to 'Grill' at 390°F for 15 minutes.
6. Flip the salmon halfway through.
7. Once done, serve the salmon with green beans.

SALMON WITH COCONUT

Prep: 12 Minutes | Cooking Time: 25 Minutes | Makes: 2 Servings

INGREDIENTS

- 2 salmon fillets, 6 ounces each
- Salt and ground black pepper, to taste
- 2 tablespoons organic butter, for frying
- ½ tablespoon red curry paste
- 1 cup of coconut cream
- ½ cup parmesan cheese, hard

DIRECTIONS

1. Mix salt, pepper, butter, red curry paste, and coconut cream in a bowl and marinate the salmon fillet in the mixture for 30 minutes.
2. Once marinated, layer a crisper tray with parchment paper and put fish fillets onto it.
3. Put the tray into the middle shelf of the air fryer.
4. Press the 'Grill' button and set the temperature to 375°F and cook for 25 minutes.
5. Flip the fillet halfway through.
6. Serve hot and enjoy with a sprinkle of parmesan cheese.

HEALTHY WHITE FISH

Prep: 10 Minutes | Cooking Time: 25 Minutes | Makes: 2 Servings

INGREDIENTS

- 2 tilapia fish fillets, 4 ounces each
- 1/4 teaspoon garlic powder
- 1 teaspoon of onion powder
- 1/3 teaspoon lemon pepper seasoning
- 1 lemon, slices round cut

- 2 tablespoons of olive oil
- ¼ cup chopped parsley, topping

DIRECTIONS

1. Coat the fish fillet with olive oil and season with garlic powder, lemon pepper, and onion powder.
2. Coat both sides well with the spices.
3. Place fillet inside grill plate and put it inside the unit.
4. Put lemon slices on top.
5. Turn the function dial to 'Grill' and set the timer to cook for 25 minutes at 390°F.
6. Once done, serve with a sprinkle of chopped parsley.

CRAB PATTIES

Prep: 15 Minutes | Cooking Time: 15 Minutes | Makes: 3 Servings

INGREDIENTS

- 1.5-pounds crab meat
- 1 tablespoon red bell pepper
- 1 tablespoon green bell pepper
- 1 tablespoon fresh parsley leaves
- 1 tablespoon mayonnaise
- 2 eggs
- 1 teaspoon Worcestershire sauce
- 2 teaspoons Old Bay seasoning

OTHER INGREDIENT

- Cooking spray, for greasing

DIRECTIONS

1. In a large mixing bowl combine all of the ingredients.
2. Make patties of the crab mixture and grease them lightly with oil spray on both sides.
3. Grease the crisper tray of the air fryer with oil spray and arrange the patties on the tray.
4. Put the tray on the bottom shelf of the air fryer.
5. Turn the function dial to 'Bake' and set it to cook for 15 minutes at 350°F.
6. Flip the patties after 5 minutes.
7. Serve with your favorite dipping sauce.

ISLAND SCALLOPS

Prep: 10 Minutes | Cooking Time: 8 Minutes | Makes: 2 Servings

Ingredients

- 1 cup coconut milk
- 12 ounces pineapple juice
- 1/4 teaspoon sea salt
- 2 tablespoons rum
- 1 pound sea scallops
- 2 cups pineapple, cubed

SALSA INGREDIENTS

- ½ cup pineapple, cubed
- ½ cup coconut flakes
- 1 large papaya, diced
- 1 avocado, diced
- 2 red onions, diced

- 2 teaspoons lime juice
- 2 tablespoons of olive oil
- Salt and black pepper, to taste
- ½ cup cilantro

DIRECTIONS

1. In a large bowl whisk coconut milk, rum, pineapple juice, and sea salt.
2. Marinate the scallops in this mixture for a few hours in the refrigerator.
3. Meanwhile, take a large bowl and mix all of the salsa ingredients.
4. Now assemble the skewers with scallops and pineapple chunks.
5. Place skewers into rotisserie holder.
6. Put inside the Air Fryer.
7. Press the 'Rotisserie' button and let the magic begin!
8. Set the timer for 8 minutes at 400°F.
9. Once done, serve with the prepared salsa.

SUNDRIED TOMATO WITH AIR-FRIED SALMON

Prep: 15 Minutes | Cooking Time: 20 Minutes | Makes: 2 Servings

INGREDIENTS

- 2 salmon fillets, 6 ounces each
- ¼ cup fresh parsley, chopped
- 4 tablespoons sun-dried tomato dressing
- Oil spray, for greasing
- Salt and black pepper, to taste
- 6 cherry tomatoes
- 1-1/2 cup broccoli, florets

DIRECTIONS

1. First, preheat the PowerXL Air Fryer Pro to 350 °F for 3 minutes.
2. Take a large bowl and mix parsley, sun-dried tomatoes dressing, salt, and pepper.
3. Coat the salmon with this mixture.
4. Lightly grease the salmon on both sides with some oil spray.
5. Put the salmon fillets into the PowerXL Air Fryer Grill Baking Pan along with the cherry tomatoes and broccoli florets.
6. Put it inside the unit.
7. Turn the function dial to 'Grill' and set it to cook for 20 minutes, at 450°F.
8. Flip fillets halfway through.
9. Once done, serve.

SALMON WITH CREAMY DILL SAUCE

Prep: 15 Minutes | Cooking Time: 20 Minutes | Makes: 2 Servings

INGREDIENTS

- 2 salmon fillets, 6 ounces each
- 1 teaspoon fresh dill
- Salt and black pepper, to taste
- Oil spray, for greasing

INGREDIENTS FOR DILL SAUCE

- 1 cup low fat plain Greek yogurt
- 1 teaspoon Dijon mustard
- 1 teaspoon lemon juice

- 2 tablespoons dill, chopped and fresh

DIRECTIONS

1. Whisk all of the sauce ingredients in a bowl. Set aside.
2. Season salmon fillet with salt, black pepper, and fresh dill.
3. Lightly spray the fillets on both sides with some oil spray.
4. Put heavy-duty foil inside the air fryer crisper tray.
5. Put the fillets inside the tray.
6. Cover the fillets with foil.
7. Place the tray inside the PowerXL Air Fryer Grill.
8. Turn the function dial to 'Grill' and set the temperature to 400°F for 20 minutes.
9. Once done, serve, and enjoy.

AIR FRYER CAJUN SCALLOPS

Prep: 8 Minutes | Cooking Time: 8 Minutes | Makes: 2 Servings

INGREDIENTS

- 10 sea scallops
- Cooking spray, for greasing
- Salt, to taste
- 1 teaspoon of Cajun seasoning, to taste
- garlic butter, melted

DIRECTIONS

1. Rinse the scallops and remove the side muscle, then rinse and pat dry with a paper towel.
2. Put the scallop in a bowl and add salt and Cajun seasoning.
3. Coat the scallops well with the mixture.
4. Lightly grease the grill plate of the PowerXL Air Fryer Grill and place the scallops inside.
5. Put it inside the unit.
6. Turn the function dial to 'Grill' and select the timer to 8 minutes at 400°F.
7. Once the scallops are cooked, transfer them to a serving plate and enjoy alongside the garlic butter dip.

AIR FRIED SCALLOPS

Prep: 15 Minutes | Cooking Time: 8 Minutes | Makes: 2 Servings

INGREDIENTS

- 8 sea scallops, cleaned and patted dry
- Salt and freshly ground black pepper, to taste
- Cooking spray, for greasing
- ¼ cup olive oil
- 2 tablespoons parsley, chopped
- 2 teaspoons capers, chopped
- 1 teaspoon lemon zest
- ½ teaspoon garlic, minced or chopped

DIRECTIONS

1. Transfer scallops to a large bowl and add salt and black pepper.
2. Coat the air fryer basket with oil spray and also coat the scallops with oil spray.
3. Transfer scallops to PowerXL Air Fryer Grill Plate and add them inside the unit, and cook at 400°F for 8 minutes.
4. Meanwhile, mix the parsley, capers, olive oil, lemon zest, lemon juice, and garlic in a bowl.
5. Drizzle the sauce over the prepared scallops and toss.
6. Serve and enjoy.

EASY AIR FRYER BREADED SEA SCALLOPS

Prep: 15 Minutes | Cooking Time: 8 Minutes | Makes: 2 Servings

INGREDIENTS

- 16 ounces of sea scallops, defrosted
- 4 teaspoons olive oil
- Salt and black pepper, to taste
- 1/2 teaspoon garlic powder
- 1/2 teaspoon onion powder
- 1/3 cup traditional breadcrumbs
- 1 teaspoon of Old Bay seasoning

DIRECTIONS

1. Take a bowl and add olive oil to it.
2. Add scallops to the olive oil and toss to coat the scallops well.
3. Take a separate bowl and mix onion powder, oil bay seasoning garlic, salt, pepper, and mix well.
4. Add breadcrumbs to a separate bowl.
5. Add scallops to the spice mixture and toss to coat the scallops well.
6. Then add the scallops to the breadcrumb bowl and coat all of the scallops well.
7. Put the grill plate inside the unit, and add scallops to it. Set the timer to 8 minutes at 400°F.
8. Shake or flip the scallops halfway through the cooking time.
9. Once the scallops are done, serve immediately.

SHRIMP LETTUCE WRAP

Prep: 20 Minutes | Cooking Time: 8 Minutes | Makes: 2 Servings

INGREDIENTS

- 10 large shrimps
- Salt and pepper
- 1/2 cup olive oil
- 1/4 cup red wine vinegar
- 2 garlic cloves minced
- 1 heaping tablespoon Italian seasoning
- 1 tablespoon lemon juice
- 2 teaspoons Dijon mustard
- 1 tablespoon Worcestershire sauce
- 5 lettuce leaves
- ½ cup ranch

DIRECTIONS

1. Whisk olive oil, salt, pepper, shrimp, red wine vinegar, minced garlic clove, Italian seasoning, lemon juice, Worcestershire sauce, and mustard.
2. Mix well and marinate shrimp in it for 2 hours in the refrigerator.
3. Take the shrimps out of the refrigerator 30 minutes before cooking.
4. Add shrimp to grill plate and add it to the air fryer, set the timer to cook for 6-8 minutes at 400°F.
5. Flip the shrimp halfway through the cooking time.
6. Once cooked, serve over lettuce leaves.
7. Enjoy with a drizzle of ranch.

EGG, SHRIMP, AND AVOCADO

Prep: 10 Minutes | Cooking Time: 10 Minutes | Makes: 3 Servings

INGREDIENTS

- 3 large avocados, pitted and cut them in half
- ¼ teaspoon of garlic salt, to taste
- Oil spray, for greasing
- 3 small organic eggs
- ¼ teaspoon of paprika powder, for sprinkling
- 6 large shrimp, finely chopped
- Chopped parsley, for topping

DIRECTIONS

1. First cut the avocadoes length-wise in half and remove the pit.
2. Scoop out the meat from the avocado and add it to a bowl.
3. In the same bowl add the shrimp and the eggs.
4. Mix well and season with garlic salt and paprika powder.
5. Scoop this mixture into the cavity of each avocado.
6. Put the avocadoes onto a greased baking pan and put the pan into the bottom of part of the PowerXL Air Fryer Grill.
7. Close the unit.
8. Turn the function dial to 'Air Fry' and set the timer to cook for 10 minutes at 400°F.
9. Once the eggs and shrimp get firm and are cooked, serve with the chopped parsley.

SHRIMP, MUSHROOM, AND BROCCOLI

Prep: 10 Minutes | Cooking Time: 8 Minutes | Makes: 2 Servings

INGREDIENTS

- 1 pound of shrimp
- 2 garlic cloves, minced
- ½ cup broccoli
- 2 tablespoons of soy sauce
- 1 teaspoon of brown sugar
- Oil spray, for greasing
- 1 tablespoon of lemon juice
- ½ pound of shitake mushroom

DIRECTIONS

1. In a large shallow bowl, mix the shrimp, garlic, broccoli, soy sauce, brown sugar, mushrooms, and lemon juice.
2. Mix all of the ingredients.
3. Take a fryer baking pan and lightly grease it with some oil spray.
4. Add the bowled ingredients to it.
5. Put the baking pan onto the bottom of the PowerXL Air Fryer Grill.
6. Turn the function dial to 'Grill' and set the timer for 8 minutes at 400°F.
7. Once cooked, serve, and enjoy.

SALMON CAKE

Prep: 20 Minutes | Cooking Time: 12 Minutes | Makes: 2 Servings

INGREDIENTS

- Cooking spray, for greasing
- 10 ounces of pink salmon
- 1 large egg
- ½ cup Panko breadcrumbs
- 2 tablespoons fresh dill, chopped
- 2 tablespoons mayonnaise
- 2 teaspoons Dijon mustard
- Salt and black pepper, to taste
- 2 lemon wedges, sliced

DIRECTIONS

1. Lightly grease the airflow rack with a few squirts of the oil spray.
2. Discard all of the bones and skin of the salmon and place it inside a medium bowl.
3. Whisk egg in a large bowl and add salmon, dill, mustard, pepper, mayonnaise, and mix well.
4. Shape into small patties with your hands.
5. Lightly coat the patties with oil spray.
6. Put the Panko breadcrumbs on a tray and coat the patties with breadcrumbs on each side.
7. Arrange the patties onto an oil-greased rack.
8. Add the rack into the air fryer.
9. Press the 'Fish' button and set the timer to cook for 12 minutes at 390 °F.
10. Flip halfway through cooking.
11. Once done, serve, and enjoy.

COCONUT SHRIMP

Prep: 20 Minutes | Cooking Time: 6 Minutes | Makes: 2 Servings

INGREDIENTS

- 10 large shrimp, raw, peeled & deveined
- 1 cup unsweetened coconut, dried
- 1 cup Panko breadcrumbs
- 2 large eggs
- 1 tablespoon corn starch
- 1 cup flour

DIRECTIONS

1. Press the 'Grill' button and preheat the PowerXL Air Fryer Grill for 5 minutes at 400°F.

2. Put the shrimp on a paper towel and pat dry after cleaning and rinsing.
3. Mix coconut flakes and breadcrumbs on a baking sheet and set them aside.
4. Crack and whisk the eggs in another bowl and set aside.
5. Mix the flour with the corn starch on a separate baking tray.
6. Dip the shrimps into the flour mixture, then in the eggs, and finally in the coconut mixture.
7. Layer parchment paper inside the air fryer crisper tray.
8. Add shrimps to the tray.
9. Insert the tray into the PowerXL Air Fryer Grill.
10. Turn the function dial to 'Grill' and set the timer to cook for 6 minutes at 375°F.
11. Once done, serve, and enjoy.

SPICY FISH FILLET

Prep: 10 Minutes | Cooking Time: 15 Minutes | Makes:1 Serving

INGREDIENTS

- 1 codfish fillet, 8 ounces
- Salt, to taste
- 1 teaspoon of lemon juice
- 1 teaspoon of red chilli flakes
- oil spray, for greasing

DIRECTIONS

1. Season fillet with salt, red chilli flakes, and lemon juice.
2. Grease the fillet with oil spray.
3. Put the fish on the air fryer grill plate.
4. Insert the plate into the unit.
5. Turn the dial to 'Air Fry' mode at 350°F for 15 minutes.
6. Once done, serve hot.

CRAB CAKES

Prep: 15 Minutes | Cooking Time: 18 Minutes | Makes: 2 Servings

INGREDIENTS

- 1 pound of crabmeat, drained
- ½ red pepper, diced small
- ¼ shallot, minced
- 1 tablespoon dijon mustard
- 1/3 cup mayonnaise
- 1/3 cup Panko Breadcrumbs
- 1 teaspoon of seafood seasoning
- 1 teaspoon freshly ground black pepper
- 1 egg, whisked

DIRECTIONS

1. Mix all the ingredients in a bowl and make patties by hand.
2. Place patties on to grill plate.
3. Place the sandwiches on the grill plate.
4. Put the grill plate on the lower shelf of the unit.
5. Turn the function dial to 'Grill' and set the temperature to 400°F, for 18 minutes.
6. Flip the patties halfway through.
7. Once done, serve and enjoy

BLACKENED SALMON

Prep: 15 Minutes | Cooking Time: 14 Minutes | Makes: 2 Servings

INGREDIENTS

- ½ side of salmon (about 1 ½ lb)
- 2 tablespoons blackened seasoning
- ½ lemon, sliced

DIRECTIONS

1. Turn the dial function to 'Grill' at 450°F for 5 minutes.
2. Let the unit preheat.
3. Now top the salmon with seasoning and let it place on the grill plate.
4. Place the pate on the lower shelf.
5. Set timer to 14 minutes.
6. Flip the fish halfway through.
7. Once it's done, serve and enjoy.

SHRIMP POPPERS

Prep: 12 Minutes | Cooking Time: 10minutes| Makes: 2 Servings

INGREDIENTS

- 1 pound of shrimp, deveined and peeled

SEASONED FLOUR

- 1/2 cup flour
- ½ tablespoon cajun seasoning
- Salt and black pepper, to taste

EGG MIXTURE INGREDIENTS

- 2 eggs
- 4 tablespoons milk
- 1 teaspoon cajun seasoning

DIRECTIONS

1. Whisk the egg in a bowl and season it with it cajun seasoning and milk.
2. Whisk it well.
3. In a separate bowl combine cajun seasoning, salt, pepper, and flour.
4. Coat the shrimp first in egg wash then in flour mixture.
5. Put the coated shrimps inside the refrigerator for 15 minutes.
6. Add shrimp to the crisper tray and insert it to the lower shelf.
7. Turn the dial to the 'Air Crisp' function and set it to 10 minutes at 375°F.
8. Once done, serve and enjoy.

Meat Recipes

Chipotle Rib Eye Steak
Page 35

Country Style Ribs
Page 36

Steak in Air Fry
Page 38

Cuban Pork Chops
Page 39

Stuffed Beef Steak Roll Up
Page 42

Spaghetti with Meatballs
Page 43

Meatballs in Tomato Sauce
Page 45

Filled Empanadas
Page 49

Grilled Lamb
Page 54

CHIPOTLE RIB EYE STEAK

Prep: 10 Minutes | Cooking Time: 10 Minutes | Makes: 2 Servings

INGREDIENTS

- 2 rib-eye steaks, 1 pound each
- Sea salt, to taste
- 1 tablespoon chipotle powder
- ½ tablespoon dark brown sugar
- 1 /2 tablespoon smoked paprika
- Pinch of cinnamon
- 1/3 teaspoon cumin
- Oil spray, for greasing

DIRECTIONS

1. Turn on the unit and preheat it for 10 minutes at 400°F.
2. First, rub the steak with sea salt and set it aside.
3. In a small bowl, mix the chipotle powder, dark brown powder, paprika, cinnamon, and cumin.
4. Rub this mixture all over the steak.
5. Grease the steak on both sides with oil spray.
6. Now put the steaks onto the grill plate of the air fryer and place the grill plate onto the lower shelf.
7. Turn the function dial to 'Grill' and adjust the timer to cook for 10 minutes at 400°F.
8. Remember to flip the steak halfway through cooking.
9. Once done, serve the steak after letting it rest for 5 minutes.

TERIYAKI GLAZED STEAK

Prep: 10 Minutes | Cooking Time: 12 Minutes | Makes: 2 Servings

INGREDIENTS

- 1 pound beef rib-eye steak

TERIYAKI GLAZE INGREDIENTS

- 1/4 cup soy sauce
- 1/3 cup Japanese cooking wine
- 1/3 cup brown sugar
- 2 tablespoons lime juice
- ½ cup orange juice
- 1/4 teaspoon Ginger, ground
- 1/6 teaspoon garlic, minced

SIDE SERVINGS

- 2 cups boiled rice

DIRECTIONS

1. Turn on the unit and preheat it for 10 minutes at 400°F.
2. In a mixing bowl, mix all of the glaze ingredients and set them aside.
3. Marinate the steak in the sauce for 1 hour in the refrigerator.
4. Afterwards, place the steak onto the air fryer grill plate and place the plate onto the middle shelf of the air fryer.
5. Turn the function dial to 'Grill' and adjust the timer to cook for 12 minutes at 370°F.

6. Flip the steak halfway through the cooking time.
7. Once done, take it out and let it rest for 10 minutes.
8. Serve over rice and enjoy.

STEAKHOUSE RIB-EYE

Prep: 12 Minutes | Cooking Time: 12 Minutes | Makes: 2 Servings

INGREDIENTS

- ½ cup butter
- ½ clove garlic
- ½ tablespoon of shallot
- ½ tablespoon parsley
- ½ tablespoon tarragon
- ½ tablespoon rosemary
- Salt, to taste
- 1 teaspoon Dijon mustard
- 1 teaspoon of lemon juice
- Freshly ground black pepper, to taste
- 1 pound rib-eye steaks
- 1 tablespoon meat rub seasoning

DIRECTIONS

1. Turn on the unit and preheat it for 10 minutes at 400°F.
2. In a bowl mix the butter, garlic, shallots, parsley, tarragon, rosemary, salt, mustard, lemon, salt, and black pepper.
3. Mix well and refrigerate in a plastic bag for a few hours.
4. Next, rub the steak with the meat rub.
5. Put the steak onto the grill plate and put the grill plate on the top shelf of the air fryer.
6. Turn the function dial to 'Air Fry' button and set the timer for 12 minutes at 400°F.
7. Flip halfway through.
8. Once done, place on a serving plate and put a few slices of the compound butter on each steak.
9. Serve once butter is slightly melted.
10. Enjoy!

COUNTRY STYLE RIBS

Prep: 10 Minutes | Cooking Time: 12 Minutes | Makes: 3 Servings

INGREDIENTS

- 16 country-style pork ribs
- 2 tablespoons cornstarch, for dusting
- 4 tablespoons olive oil
- 3 teaspoons dry mustard
- 2 teaspoons thyme
- 2 teaspoons garlic powder
- 2 teaspoons dried marjoram
- Salt and black pepper, to taste

DIRECTIONS

1. Turn on the unit and preheat it for 10 minutes at 400°F.
2. Take a bowl and combine oil, dry mustard, thyme powder, garlic, marjoram, salt, and black pepper.
3. Dust the steak with cornstarch.

4. Let it sit in a refrigerator for 30 minutes.
5. Afterwards, put the steak onto the grill plate.
6. Put the grill plate on the top shelf of the air fryer.
7. Turn the function dial to 'Grill', and set the timer for 12 minutes at 400°F.
8. Flip halfway through cooking.
9. Once done, place on serving plate.
10. Serve and enjoy.

CHINESE SPARE RIB

Prep: 15 Minutes | Cooking Time: 14 Minutes | Makes: 3 Servings

Ingredients

- 4 teaspoons hoisin sauce
- 4 teaspoons ketchup
- 4 teaspoons honey
- 1 teaspoon sake
- 1 teaspoon rice vinegar
- 1/2 teaspoon ginger
- 2 cloves of garlic
- ¼ teaspoon Chinese five-spice powder
- Salt, to taste
- 3 teaspoons sweet chilli sauce
- 2 pounds pork spares ribs, boneless

DIRECTIONS

1. Turn on the unit and preheat it for 10 minutes at 450°F.
2. Mix all of the marinade ingredients in a bowl and stir.
3. Marinate the rib in this mixture for 1 hour.
4. Place the pork rib on to grill plate and adjust the plate on the middle shelf.
5. Turn the function dial to 'Grill' and set the timer for 14 minutes at 400°F.
6. Brush the rib with the marinade after every 4 minutes of cooking.
7. Once done, remove and serve once slightly cooled down.

GLAZED STEAK RECIPE

Prep: 15 Minutes | Cooking Time: 12 Minutes | Makes: 2 Servings

INGREDIENTS

- 1 pound of beef steaks
- ½ cup, soy sauce
- Black pepper, to taste
- 1 tablespoon of olive oil
- 1 teaspoon of grated ginger
- 4 cloves of garlic, minced
- 1/4 cup dark brown sugar
- 2 tablespoons of garlic butter, solid

DIRECTIONS

1. Turn on the unit and preheat it for 10 minutes at 400°F.
2. Whisk soy sauce, olive oil, ginger, garlic, dark brown sugar, and black pepper in a bowl.
3. Rub this mixture all over the steak.

4. Marinate the steak in the refrigerator for 30 minutes.
5. Afterward, grease the steak on both sides with oil spray.
6. Place the steaks on the baking pan and place the pan at the bottom of the unit.
7. Set the timer for 12 minutes at 375°F.
8. Flip the steaks halfway through.
9. Take out the steaks and put garlic butter on top.
10. Let the butter melt and then serve hot.
11. Enjoy!

STEAK IN AIR FRY

Prep: 15 Minutes | Cooking Time: 10 Minutes | Makes: 3 Servings

INGREDIENTS

- 1 teaspoon of canola oil
- 2 tablespoons of Montreal steak seasoning
- 1.5-pounds of beef steak, rib-eye

DIRECTIONS

1. Turn on the unit and preheat it for 10 minutes at 400°F.
2. Rub the steak with canola oil and season well with the Montreal steak seasoning.
3. Arrange the steak on a grill plate and place it on the bottom shelf of the air fryer.
4. Adjust the timer to 10 minutes at 400°F.
5. Remember to flip halfway through.
6. Once done, serve.

BBQ RIBS

Prep: 15 Minutes | Cooking Time: 30 Minutes | Makes: 4 Servings

INGREDIENTS

- 4 tablespoons of barbecue spice rub
- 1 tablespoon kosher salt and black pepper
- 3 tablespoons brown sugar
- 2 pounds pork spares ribs, boneless
- 1 cup barbecue sauce
- Oil spray, for greasing

DIRECTIONS

1. Turn on the unit and preheat it for 10 minutes at 400°F.
2. Combine salt, black pepper, BBQ spice rub, and brown sugar in a bowl and mix well.
3. Lightly spray the ribs with oil and then rub the spice mixture all over the rib.
4. Thread the pork ribs onto two skewers and assemble the skewer racks within the rotisserie shaft, and at the end, secure the shaft.
5. Lock into the adjustable skewer racks.
6. Set the racks into the unit sockets.
7. Now press the 'Rotisserie' button and set the timer to cook for 30 minutes at 400°F.

8. Brush the ribs with BBQ sauce after every 10 minutes of cooking.
9. Once done, remove and serve once slightly cooled down.

BEEF RIBS

Prep: 15 Minutes | Cooking Time: 30 Minutes | Makes: 2 Servings

INGREDIENTS FOR MARINADE

- ¼ cup olive oil
- 4 garlic cloves, minced
- ½ cup white wine vinegar
- ¼ cup soy sauce, reduced-sodium
- ¼ cup Worcestershire sauce
- 1 lemon juice
- Salt and black pepper, to taste
- 2 tablespoons of Italian seasoning
- 1 teaspoon of smoked paprika
- 2 tablespoons of mustard
- ½ cup maple syrup

MEAT INGREDIENTS

- Oil spray, for greasing
- 1.5-pound of beef ribs lean

DIRECTIONS

1. Turn on the unit and preheat it for 10 minutes at 400°F.
2. Take a mixing bowl and mix all of the marinade ingredients.
3. Add ribs to the marinade and transfer it to a zip lock bag.
4. Put the bag in the refrigerator for 4 hours.
5. Now take out the ribs and place them into an air fryer baking pan lined with aluminium foil.
6. Adjust the pan inside the unit.
7. Press the 'Power' button and set the timer for 30 minutes at 400 °F.
8. Flip the ribs halfway through cooking.
9. Once done, serve the juicy and tender ribs.
10. Enjoy!

CUBAN PORK CHOPS

Prep: 15 Minutes | Cooking Time: 20 Minutes | Makes: 4 Servings

INGREDIENTS

- ½ cup mango nectar
- 1 lime, juice, and zest
- ¼ cup of olive oil
- 2 cloves of garlic
- Salt and black pepper, to taste
- ¼ teaspoon cumin
- ¼ cup cilantro
- 2-pounds boneless pork chops
- 2 tablespoons butter, organic
- 1 tablespoon flour

DIRECTIONS

1. Turn on the unit and preheat it for 10 minutes at 400°F.
2. Combine the mango nectar, lime juice, olive oil, garlic, salt, black pepper, cumin, and cilantro in a bowl and mix well.

3. Marinate the pork chops in this mixture for a few hours.
4. Put the chops onto a grill plate, and put the grill plate on the lower or middle rack of the air fryer.
5. Turn the function dial to 'Grill' and set the timer for 14 minutes at 400°F.
6. Rotate the rack after 6 minutes of cooking.
7. Add the leftover marinated sauce to a saucepan and cook until thickened.
8. Whisk flour with butter and add it to the sauce.
9. Plate the cooked pork chops and pour the sauce over them.
10. Serve and enjoy.

SPICY LAMB CHOPS

Prep: 20 Minutes | Cooking Time: 15 minutes | Makes: 4 Servings

INGREDIENTS

- 2 pounds of lamb chops, bone-in
- Salt and black pepper, to taste
- 1 teaspoon of lemon zest
- ½ tablespoon of lemon juice
- ½ teaspoon of paprika
- 1 teaspoon of garlic powder
- 1 teaspoon of Italian seasoning
- 1/2 teaspoon of onion powder
- Oil spray for greasing

DIRECTIONS

1. Turn on the unit and preheat it for 10 minutes at 400°F.
2. Put the lamb chops into a large bowl and combine with all of the other ingredients.
3. Rub the chops well, and let it marinate for 2 hours in the refrigerator.
4. Then take out the chops and grease them with oil spray.
5. Put the chops onto the grill plate and put them on the lower shelf of the air fryer.
6. Turn the function dial to 'Grill' and set the timer to cook for 15 minutes at 400°F.
7. Once done, serve.
8. Enjoy!

YOGURT LAMB CHOPS

Prep: 20 Minutes | Cooking Time: 16 Minutes | Makes: 4 Servings

INGREDIENTS

2 cups plain Greek yogurt
1 lemon, juice only
1 teaspoon ground cumin
1 teaspoon ground coriander
Pinch of turmeric
½ teaspoon ground allspice
2 pounds rib lamb chops (1–1¼ inches thick cut)
3 tablespoons olive oil, divided

DIRECTIONS

1. Turn on the unit and preheat it for 10 minutes at 400°F.
2. Add the pork chop along with all other ingredients to a bowl.
3. Marinate for 2 hours in the refrigerator.
4. Afterward, take out the lamb chops.
5. Layer the air fryer baking pan with aluminium foil.
6. Put the chops inside the pan, and place the pan inside the air fryer.
7. Set the timer for 16 minutes at 400°F.
8. Flip the chops halfway through.
9. Once done, serve, and enjoy.

CLASSIC PORK CHOPS

Prep: 20 Minutes | Cooking Time: 15 Minutes | Makes: 3 Servings

INGREDIENTS

- A handful of rosemary leaves, chopped
- Salt and black pepper, to taste
- 2 garlic cloves
- 1-inch ginger
- 2 tablespoons of olive oil
- 10 pork chops

DIRECTIONS

1. Turn on the unit and preheat it for 10 minutes at 400°F.
2. Put ginger, garlic, olive oil, rosemary leaves, salt, and pepper in a blender and pulse it well.
3. Rub this paste over the pork chops and let it rest for 1 hour in the refrigerator.
4. Put the chops onto the grill plate, and put them on the lower parts of the air fryer.
5. Turn the function dial to 'Grill' and set the timer to cook for 14 minutes at 400°F.
6. Rotate the chops after 7 minutes of cooking.
7. Serve.

TASTY AND EASY PORK CHOPS

Prep: 20 Minutes | Cooking Time: 14 Minutes | Makes: 2 Servings

INGREDIENTS

- 1 tablespoon dry mustard powder
- ¼ cup brown sugar, packed
- 1/3 cup bourbon
- 3 tablespoons Worcestershire sauce
- ¼ cup of soy sauce
- ¼ cup apple cider vinegar
- Salt and pepper to taste
- 6 boneless pork chops

DIRECTIONS

1. Turn on the unit and preheat it for 10 minutes at 400°F.
2. Mix all of the marinade ingredients in a bowl and marinate the pork chops in it.

3. Let it sit in the refrigerator for 1 hour.
4. Then put the chops onto the grill plate, and adjust the grill plate on the middle shelf of the air fryer.
5. Turn the function dial to 'Grill' set the timer to cook for 14 minutes at 400°F.
6. Serve.

CHINESE BBQ PORK

Prep: 15 Minutes | Cooking Time: 20 Minutes | Makes: 4 Servings

SAUCE INGREDIENTS

- 6 tablespoons of soy sauce
- ½ cup red wine
- 4 tablespoons of oyster sauce
- 1 tablespoon of hoisin sauce
- 1/3 cup honey
- ¼ cup dark brown sugar
- 1 teaspoon of ginger-garlic, paste
- 1 teaspoon of five-spice powder
- Salt and black pepper, to taste

OTHER INGREDIENTS

- 2 pounds of pork chops

DIRECTIONS

1. Turn on the unit and preheat it for 10 minutes at 400°F.
2. Mix all of the sauce ingredients in a bowl and whisk well.
3. Transfer half of the sauce to a saucepan and simmer on low until it gets thickened.
4. Set aside.
5. Marinate the chop in the remaining sauce and let it sit in the refrigerator for 1 hour.
6. Afterwards, put the pork slices onto the grill plate and place the grill plate at the bottom shelf of the air fryer.
7. Turn the function dial to 'Grill' and set the timer to cook for 14 minutes at 400°F.
8. Rotate the grill plate after 7 minutes of cooking and baste with the sauce from the saucepan.
9. Once done, serve the pork chop.

STUFFED BEEF STEAK ROLL UP

Prep: 15 Minutes | Cooking Time: 15 Minutes | Makes: 2 Servings

INGREDIENTS

- 500 grams beef steaks
- 4 tablespoons pesto
- 10 slices of Provolone cheese
- 1/3 cup roasted red bell peppers
- 1-1/3 cup fresh spinach
- Salt and black pepper, to taste
- Oil spray, for greasing

DIRECTIONS

1. Turn on the unit and preheat it for 10 minutes at 400°F.
2. Spread the pesto evenly over the beefsteak and then layer with the bell pepper, cheese, and spinach.

3. Roll the meat and secure the ends with a toothpick.
4. Season with salt and black pepper and lightly grease with oil spray.
5. Put onto the grill plate and place the grill plate on the bottom shelf of the air fryer.
6. Turn the function dial to the 'Steaks/Chops' button and set the timer for 14 minutes at 400°F.
7. Flip halfway through the cooking time.
8. Once finished, take it out and let it rest for 10 minutes before cutting and serving.

SPANISH RUB PORK BURGERS

Prep: 25 Minutes | Cooking Time: 18 Minutes | Makes: 4 Servings

INGREDIENTS

RUB INGREDIENTS

- ½ tablespoon smoked paprika
- 1 teaspoon cumin
- Salt and black pepper, to taste
- 2 teaspoons dried cilantro

OTHER INGREDIENTS

- 1 pound ground pork
- 4 hamburger buns
- 2 tablespoons of butter
- Citrus Cilantro Dressing, as needed
- Tomato slices, as needed

DIRECTIONS

1. Turn on the unit and preheat it for 10 minutes at 400°F.
2. Combine all of the listed rub ingredients in a bowl and add ground pork.
3. Make into small patties with your hands and set them aside in the refrigerator to firm up.
4. Place patties onto the grill plate and adjust the grill plate into the middle shelf of the air fryer.
5. Turn the Function dial to 'Grill' and set the timer for 14 minutes at 400°F.
6. Flip halfway through.
7. Now take out the patties and place buns on the racks.
8. Cook for 3 minutes at 370 °F.
9. Cut buns and spread butter on each side.
10. Put patties on top along with cilantro dressing and tomato slices.
11. Serve by placing another bun on top to make a burger.

SPAGHETTI WITH MEATBALLS

Prep: 15 Minutes | Cooking Time: 22-25 Minutes | Makes: 2 Servings

INGREDIENTS

- 1 pound ground beef
- 4 cups marinara sauce
- Salt and pepper to taste
- 1 pound spaghetti, cooked
- 1 cup grated parmesan cheese

- 2 tablespoons of olive oil
- 1 tablespoon of onion powder
- ¼ teaspoon of red chilli flakes

DIRECTIONS

1. Cook spaghetti in boiling water according to package instruction, then drain and set aside.
2. Take a bowl and add salt, onion powder, pepper, and red chillies along with ground meat.
3. Mix well and make into meatballs with your hands.
4. Place the meatballs in the air fryer baking pan and place the pan inside the air fryer.
5. Turn the function dial to 'Grill' and set the timer for 18 minutes at 400°F.
6. Meanwhile, heat oil in a pan and add marinara sauce.
7. Cook for 2 minutes.
8. Add cooked meatballs to the sauce and top with parmesan cheese.
9. Serve over cooked spaghetti.
10. Enjoy hot.

HAM BURGER PATTIES

Prep: 25 Minutes | Cooking Time: 16 Minutes | Makes: 2 Servings

INGREDIENTS

- 1 pound of ground beef
- Salt and pepper, to taste
- ½ teaspoon of red chilli powder
- ¼ teaspoon of coriander powder
- 2 tablespoons of chopped onion
- 1 green chilli, chopped
- Oil spray for greasing

TOPPINGS:

- 2-3 buns, toasted
- 4 slices of cheddar cheese
- 4 slices of tomato
- Iceberg lettuce, torn pieces
- Ketchup, as needed
- Mayonnaise, as needed

DIRECTIONS

1. Take a bowl and add all of the ingredients to it.
2. Mix well and make into burger patties with wet hands.
3. Spray patties on both sides with oil spray.
4. Put patties onto the baking pan.
5. Put baking pan on the middle shelf of the air fryer.
6. Turn the function dial to 'Grill' and set the timer for 16 minutes at 400°F.
7. Flip halfway through cooking.
8. Once done, serve by placing on a toasted bun and adding all of the topping ingredients.

MEATBALLS IN TOMATO SAUCE

Prep: 25 Minutes | Cooking Time: 25 Minutes | Makes: 4 Servings

INGREDIENTS

- 1 green onion, minced
- 2 teaspoons of garlic, minced
- 1 egg, cooked
- 1/4 cup saltine cracker crumbs
- Salt and black pepper, to taste
- 1-1/4 pound beef, ground
- Oil spray, for greasing
- 2.5 cups pasta sauce
- 1 teaspoon of mustard paste
- 2 green chillies
- ¼ cup chopped parsley
- 1 cup parmesan cheese
- 2 cups cooked pasta

DIRECTIONS

1. Take a bowl and mix green onions, garlic cloves, cooked egg, cracker crumbs, salt, pepper, beef, and green chillies.
2. Form into meatballs.
3. Lightly coat the meatballs with some oil spray.
4. Place the meatballs into the air fryer baking pan and place the pan inside the air fryer.
5. Press the 'Power' button and set the timer for 16 minutes at 400°F.
6. Shake the pan halfway through the cooking time.
7. Meanwhile, combine pasta sauce and mustard paste in a saucepan and cook for a few minutes until it starts to bubble.
8. Add the cooked meatballs to the pasta sauce and let it simmer for 1 minute.
9. Add chopped parsley on top.
10. Now pour this over cooked pasta and sprinkle parmesan cheese over the top.
11. Enjoy hot.

TURKEY PANINI

Prep: 15 Minutes | Cooking Time: 22-25 Minutes | Makes: 2 Servings

INGREDIENTS

- 10 strips of bacon
- 4 slices white bread
- ¼ cup ranch dressing
- 10-ounce deli-sliced turkey breast
- 4 slices American cheese
- 2 teaspoons salted butter

DIRECTIONS

1. Layer the bacon strips onto the grill plate and place the plate into the bottom of the air fryer.
2. Press the 'Power' button and then press the 'Air Fryer' button.
3. Cook at 400°F for 14 minutes.
4. Remember to rotate the grill plate halfway through the cooking time.
5. Once done, take it out and set aside.
6. Butter one side of each bread slice.
7. Place two bread slices, butter side down on a crisper tray.

8. Top with ranch dressing and turkey, cooked bacon slices, and American cheese on each slice of bread.
9. Top the sandwiches with the two remaining bread slices, butter side up.
10. Put the crisper tray on the middle shelf of the unit.
11. Turn the function dial to 'Grill', and then press the 'Air Fry' button.
12. Set it to 400°F for 8 minutes, flipping halfway through.
13. Serve hot.

PORK MILANESE AND CHEESY STUFFED MUSHROOMS

Prep: 20 Minutes | Cooking Time: 26-28 Minutes | Makes: 2 Servings

INGREDIENTS

- 2 eggs, beaten
- 2 cups seasoned breadcrumbs
- 6 thin-sliced boneless pork chops
- 8-ounce cream cheese
- 1 cup sour cream
- 1 cup baby spinach, chopped
- ½ teaspoon garlic powder
- 1/4 teaspoon salt
- 1/4 teaspoon pepper
- 6 medium-sized Portobello caps
- 1 or 1/3 cup mozzarella cheese, shredded

DIRECTIONS

1. Crack eggs in a bowl and set them aside.
2. In a separate baking tray or pan add breadcrumbs.
3. Dip chops first in eggs then in breadcrumb mixture.
4. Place the pork onto a PowerXL Air Fryer Grill Plate and add it to lower shelf of unit.
5. Press the 'Power' button and set the timer to cook for 16 minutes at 375°F.
6. Remember to flip the chops halfway through.
7. Once done take it out and let it cool for a while.
8. Meanwhile, mix cream cheese, spinach, sour cream, garlic powder, salt, and pepper in a bowl and fill the cavity of the mushrooms with it.
9. Place the mushroom onto the PowerXL Air Fryer Baking Pan.
10. Turn the function dial to bake and set the temperature to 370°F for 10 minutes.
11. Once done, serve with the steak.

MOJITO LAMB RIBS

Prep: 15 Minutes | Cooking Time: 30 Minutes | Makes: 4 Servings

INGREDIENTS

- 4 limes, divided
- 1/3 cup olive oil
- 1/4 cup fresh mint, chopped
- 8 large cloves of garlic, minced
- Salt, to taste
- ½ teaspoon pepper
- 12 lamb ribs chops, trimmed

DIRECTIONS

1. Combine olive oil, lime zest, lime juice, mint, salt, garlic, and pepper in a bowl and mix well.
2. Rub the lamb with the spice blend.
3. Marinate the lamb for 2 hours.
4. Skewer the lamb chops onto a skewer.
5. Thread the lamb ribs onto two skewers and then assemble the skewer rack with the rotisserie shaft and secure the shaft.
6. Lock it into the Adjustable Skewer racks.
7. Set the racks into the unit sockets.
8. Now press the 'Rotisserie' button and set the timer to 30 minutes at 400°F.
9. Once done, remove and serve once slightly cooled down.

SKIRT STEAK WITH BALSAMIC SHALLOTS

Prep: 15 Minutes | Cooking Time: 20 Minutes | Makes: 2 Servings

INGREDIENTS

MARINADE INGREDIENTS

- ¼ cup balsamic vinegar
- 2 teaspoons brown sugar
- Salt and black pepper, to taste
- 2 cloves of garlic, chopped
- ½ teaspoon of olive oil

STEAK INGREDIENTS

- 1 pound skirt steak
- 10 shallots, peeled

DIRECTIONS

1. Turn on the unit and preheat it for 10 minutes at 400°F.
2. Mix all of the marinade ingredients in a bowl.
3. Marinate the steak and shallots in the marinade for 30 minutes in a refrigerator.
4. Take out the steak and shallots from the marinade and arrange them onto a grill plate.
5. Turn the function dial to 'Bake' and set the timer to 20 minutes at 400°F.
6. Remember to flip halfway through.
7. Take out and cool for 10 minutes before serving.

AIR FRY LOIN LAMB CHOPS

Prep: 12 Minutes | Cooking Time: 15 Minutes | Makes: 3 Servings

INGREDIENTS

- 4 cloves of garlic, sliced
- 1 tablespoon minced rosemary leaves
- 2 teaspoons red wine vinegar
- 2 tablespoons soy sauce
- 3 tablespoons olive oil
- 6-8 loin lamb chops, 1 ½ in. thick

DIRECTIONS

1. Turn on the unit and preheat it for 10 minutes at 400°F.
2. Take a bowl and mix rosemary leaves, garlic, red wine vinegar, soy sauce, and olive oil to make a marinade.
3. Marinade the lamb chops for 2 hours and place in the refrigerator.
4. Afterward, put the chops onto the airflow racks, and place the racks on the middle, and bottom shelves.
5. Turn the function dial to 'Grill' and set the timer to cook for 15 minutes at 370°F.
6. Rotate the rack after 7 minutes of cooking.
7. Once done, serve.

ASIAN PORK CHOPS

Prep: 10 Minutes | Cooking Time: 14 Minutes | Makes: 2 Servings

INGREDIENTS

1 pound pork spare ribs
¼ cup apple cider vinegar
½ cup of soy sauce
2 teaspoon onion powder
1 teaspoon garlic powder
¼ cup hoisin sauce
Salt, to taste (optional)

DIRECTIONS

1. Turn on the unit and preheat it for 10 minutes at 400°F.
2. Add all of the listed ingredients to a large bowl.
3. Add pork chops and transfer to the refrigerator for 1 hour.
4. Afterwards, put the chops onto the grill plate and place the racks on the middle, and bottom shelves of the PowerXL Air Fryer Grill.
5. Turn the function dial to 'Grill' and set the timer to cook for 14 minutes at 400°F.
6. Rotate the rack after 7 minutes of cooking.
7. Once done, serve.

AIR FRYER STEAK

Prep: 12 Minutes | Cooking Time: 12 Minutes | Makes: 2 Servings

Ingredients

- 1.3 pounds of steak (Rib eye)

Ingredients for Steak Marinade

- 1 teaspoon olive oil
- Salt and black pepper, to taste
- 1/2 teaspoon dried garlic powder
- 1/2 teaspoon dried onion powder
- 1 teaspoon Montreal Steak Seasoning
- 1/8 teaspoon cayenne pepper

DIRECTIONS

1. Turn on the unit and preheat it for 10 minutes at 400°F at 'Grill' mode.

2. Put the steak marinade ingredients in a bowl and mix well with a fork.
3. Add the steak and let the steak coat well in the marinade.
4. Let the steak sit in the refrigerator for 2 hours.
5. Place the steak on the grill plate and adjust it at the bottom shelf and of the PowerXL Air Fryer Grill.
6. Set the timer for 12 minutes at 400°F and turn the function dial to 'Grill' mode.
7. Flip the steak halfway through cooking.
8. Take out the steak and let it sit and rest for 10 minutes before serving.
9. Enjoy.

RUMP STEAK

Prep: 12 Minutes | Cooking Time: 14 Minutes | Makes: 2 Servings

INGREDIENTS

- 1 pound of rump steak
- 1 tablespoon of steak seasoning
- 1 tablespoon of olive oil

DIRECTIONS

1. Turn on the unit and preheat it for 10 minutes at 400°F.
2. Rub the steak with the steak seasoning and drizzle olive oil all over the steak, rubbing generously all over.
3. Put the steak onto the grill plate and adjust the plate onto the middle shelf.
4. Turn the function dial to 'Grill' and set the timer to 14 minutes at 400°F.
5. After 7 minutes, flip the steak.
6. Continue with the cooking.
7. Let the steak sit for 5 minutes before serving.

FILLED EMPANADAS

Prep: 15 Minutes | Cooking Time: 20 Minutes | Makes: 3-4 Servings

INGREDIENTS

- 450 grams minced beef
- 450 grams puff pastry
- 1 tablespoon olive oil
- 1 green pepper, diced
- 1 onion, peeled and chopped
- 2 garlic clove, peeled and chopped
- ½ teaspoon cumin
- 1 cup tomato sauce
- Sea salt and pepper, to taste
- 2 egg yolks
- 1 tablespoon full-fat milk

DIRECTIONS

1. Add the olive oil to a pan and the minced beef and cook for 5 minutes.
2. Drain excess liquid.
3. Add garlic and cook until there is an aroma.
4. Then add the listed ingredients except for the milk, egg yolks, and pastry.
5. Let all ingredients cook on a low heat for 12 minutes.

6. Let it cooled by setting it aside.
7. Now lay pastry pockets on a flat surface and add the cooked mixture at one end.
8. Brush the pastry with egg to seal the edges with the help of a fork.
9. Continue to fill all pastry pockets.
10. Now arrange the pastries in the air fryer baking pan.
11. Place the pan inside the unit.
12. Turn the function dial to 'Bake' and set it to cook for 15-20 minutes at 350°F.
13. Once the pastry gets puffy, serve, and enjoy.

SUGAR GLAZE HAM

Prep: 10 Minutes | Cooking Time: 30 Minutes | Makes: 2 Servings

INGREDIENTS

- 1 pound of ham
- 1/3 cup orange juice
- 2 tablespoons brown sugar
- Pinch of cloves, powdered

DIRECTIONS

1. Take a bowl and mix cloves powder, brown sugar, and orange juice.
2. Place the rotisserie shaft in the middle of the ham, securing the shaft.
3. Lock it into the Adjustable Skewer racks.
4. Set the racks into the air fryer sockets.
5. Turn the function dial to the 'Rotisserie' button and set the timer to 30 minutes at 400°F.
6. Brush the ham with marinade after every 5 minutes.
7. Once done, remove and serve once slightly cooled down.

CORNED BEEF AND CABBAGE ROLLS

Prep: 10 Minutes | Cooking Time: 6 Minutes | Makes: 4 Servings

INGREDIENTS

- 8 egg rolls
- 1 pound corned beef, shredded
- 1 cup red cabbage, thinly sliced
- 6 tablespoons of spicy mustard, as needed

DIRECTIONS

1. Layer the egg roll on a flat work surface and place a tablespoon of corned beef and some mustard.
2. Wrap to form a spring roll.
3. Seal the edges with water.
4. Prepare all of the rolls.
5. Grease the rolls with oil spray.
6. Layer the eggrolls on the crisper tray of the unit.
7. Adjust it on the middle of the PowerXL Air Fryer Grill.
8. Cook for 6 minutes at 400°F at 'Air Fry' mode.
9. Remember to flip halfway through.
10. Once done, serve.

MINTY PORK CHOPS

Prep: 10 Minutes | Cooking Time: 15 Minutes | Makes: 4 Servings

INGREDIENTS

- 1 tablespoon of lemon juice
- 1 cup Greek yogurt
- Salt and black pepper, to taste
- ½ teaspoon of ginger-garlic paste
- 1/2 cup fresh mint, grated
- 12 lamb chops

DIRECTIONS

1. Turn on the unit and preheat it for 10 minutes at 450°F at 'Grill' mode.
2. Combine Greek yogurt, lemon juice, salt, pepper, garlic, and ginger paste in a bowl.
3. Add chopped mint.
4. Marinate chops in a bowl marinade for 2 hours in the refrigerator.
5. Place chops into the air fryer grill plate lined with aluminium foil.
6. Press the 'Power' button and set the timer 400°F at 'Grill' mode.
7. Flip the chops halfway through.
8. Once done, serve

SALT AND BLACK PEPPER STEAK

Prep: 10 Minutes | Cooking Time: 10 Minutes | Makes: 2 Servings

INGREDIENTS

- 2 sirloin steaks, 1.5-pounds
- Salt and black pepper, to taste
- 4 tablespoons of melted butter

DIRECTIONS

1. Turn on the unit and preheat it for 10 minutes at 450°F at 'Grill' mode.
2. Rub the steak with butter, salt, and black pepper.
3. Grease the airflow racks of the air fryer with oil spray.
4. Arrange the steak onto the grill plate and place it on the bottom shelf of the air fryer.
5. Adjust the timer to 10 minutes at 400°F.
6. Remember to flip halfway through.
7. Once done, serve.

MUSTARD PORK CHOPS

Prep: 15 Minutes | Cooking Time: 14 Minutes | Makes: 2 Servings

INGREDIENTS

- 6 boneless pork chops, ¾-1" thick
- 2 teaspoons of olive oil
- 1/2 cup Parmesan cheese, grated
- 1 teaspoon of paprika powder
- 1 teaspoon of garlic powder
- 1 teaspoon onion powder
- 2 teaspoons mustard powder
- Salt and black pepper, to taste

DIRECTIONS

1. Turn on the unit and preheat it for 10 minutes at 450°F at 'Grill' mode.
2. Take a bowl and mix parmesan cheese, olive oil, paprika, garlic powder, mustard powder, onion powder, salt, and black pepper.
3. Dredge the chops in the parmesan mixture and place them into the grill plate lined with parchment paper.
4. Place inside the PowerXL Air Fryer Grill.
5. Turn the function dial to 'Grill'.
6. Adjust the temperature to 14 minutes at 400°F.
7. Flip the chops halfway through.
8. Once done, serve, and enjoy.

BELL PEPPERS WITH SAUSAGES

Prep: 10 Minutes | Cooking Time: 20 Minutes | Makes: 2 Servings

INGREDIENTS

- 1 pound of beef sausages
- 2 green bell peppers, whole
- Oil spray, for greasing
- 1 cup of sour cream
- 1 cup cooked rice

DIRECTIONS

1. Preheat the air fryer by pressing the 'Power' button and setting the temperature at 450°F for 10 minutes.
2. Place sausages accompanied by bell peppers into a lightly-greased air fryer baking pan.
3. Now place the pan inside the unit and set it to cook for 20 minutes at 375°F.
4. Once done serve over cooked rice with a dollop of sour cream.

PORK CHOP WITH RASPBERRY CHIPOTLE SAUCE

Prep: 20 Minutes | Cooking Time: 18 Minutes | Makes: 3 Servings

INGREDIENTS

SAUCE INGREDIENTS

- 12 ounces raspberry-chipotle sauce
- ¼ cup soy sauce
- 1 tablespoon honey
- 2 garlic cloves, finely chopped
- 1 teaspoon garlic powder
- Salt, to taste

OTHER INGREDIENTS

- 1.5-pounds of pork chops

DIRECTIONS

1. Turn on the unit and preheat it for 10 minutes at 450°F at 'Grill' mode.
2. Take a bowl and mix all of the listed sauce ingredients.
3. Put the pork chops in the mixture and coat well with this mixture.

4. Let it sit in the refrigerator for 2 hours.
5. Put chops inside the air fryer baking pan lined with parchment paper.
6. Turn the function dial to 'Grill' and set it to cook for 15-18 minutes at 400°F.
7. Flip chops halfway through.
8. Once done, serve

EASY PORK CHOPS

Prep: 20 Minutes | Cooking Time: 18 Minutes | Makes: 2 Servings

INGREDIENTS

- 4 pork chops
- 1 tablespoon of old bay seasoning
- 3 eggs, whisked
- 1 cup milk
- 2 cups cornmeal
- Salt and black pepper, to taste
- 2 cups all-purpose flour

DIRECTIONS

1. Turn on the unit and preheat it for 10 minutes at 450°F at 'Grill' mode.
2. First, mix eggs with milk and whisk well.
3. In a separate bowl add the cornmeal and flour.
4. Add salt, pepper, and old bay seasoning to the flour.
5. Now dredge the pork chops in egg wash and then add into the flour mixture.
6. Coat the pork chops well and arrange them on the grill plate.

7. Put inside the air fryer on the middle shelf.
8. Turn the function dial to 'Grill' and adjust the temperature to 450°F and cook for 18 minutes.
9. Flip chops halfway through.
10. Once done, serve, and enjoy.

PORK CHOPS WITH BASIL-GARLIC RUB

Prep: 15 Minutes | Cooking Time: 18 Minutes | Makes: 2 Servings

INGREDIENTS

- 6 pork chops
- 6 cloves of garlic
- ½ cup fresh basil
- 4 tablespoons lemon juice
- 4 tablespoons extra virgin olive oil
- Salt and black pepper, to taste

DIRECTIONS

1. Turn on the unit and preheat it for 10 minutes at 450°F at 'Grill' mode.
2. Blend garlic cloves, basil, lemon juice, and olive oil in a blender, and add salt and black pepper.
3. Transfer to a bowl and rub the pork chops with the blend.
4. Arrange pork chops onto the grill plate and put the plate on the middle shelf of the air fryer.
5. Adjust the temperature to 400 °F and cook for 18 minutes by turning the function dial to 'Grill'.
6. Flip chops halfway through.

7. Once done, serve, and enjoy.

BRINED PORK CHOPS

Prep: 15 Minutes | Cooking Time: 14 Minutes | Makes: 2 Servings

INGREDIENTS

1 quart water
1 small onion, thinly sliced
4 sprigs of thyme
3 sprigs of rosemary
4 cloves of garlic, smashed flat with the back of a knife
Salt, to taste
4 tablespoons molasses
4 allspice berries
2 cloves
2 bags orange pekoe tea, Lipton
6 bone-in pork loin chops, 12 ounces each

DIRECTIONS

1. Turn on the unit and preheat it for 10 minutes at 450°F at 'Grill' mode.
2. In a large pot pour water and add thyme, onion, rosemary, garlic, molasses, salt, allspice berries, tea bag, and cloves.
3. Bring to boil and then set aside to cool completely.
4. Remove tea bags and add pork chops to the pot.
5. Marinate pork chops for 24 hours.
6. After 24 hours, remove the pork chops and pat dry with a paper towel.
7. Once dry arrange onto the grill plate and place it on the middle shelf of the air fryer.
8. Turn the function dial to 'Grill' and cook for 14 minutes at 450°F.
9. Flip pork chops halfway through the cooking time.
10. Once done, serve.

GRILLED LAMB RECIPES

Prep: 20 Minutes | Cooking Time: 16 Minutes | Makes: 2 Servings

INGREDIENTS

- 1 cup salsa
- 1/3 cup chopped onion
- 1/3 cup molasses
- 1/4 cup fresh lime juice
- 1/3 cup chicken broth
- 3 garlic cloves, minced
- 4 tablespoons jalapeno peppers, chopped seeded
- 2 teaspoons brown sugar
- 4 lamb chops
- 1 cup sour cream, as needed

DIRECTIONS

1. Combine salsa, lime juice, molasses broth, garlic, sugar, jalapeno pepper, and onion in a saucepan and simmer on a low heat for 10 minutes.
2. Rub the lamb chops with salt and pepper, and grease chops with oil spray on both sides.

3. Place the chops on the grill plate and cook for 16 minutes at 400°F at the 'Grill' function.
4. Flip halfway through.
5. Baste the chops with the prepared sauce every 10 minutes.

STEAK STRIPS

Prep: 15 Minutes | Cooking Time: 15 Minutes | Makes: 2 Servings

INGREDIENTS

- 1 pound of thin skirt steak
- 1/2 cup soy sauce
- 1/8 teaspoon of ground clove
- ¼ teaspoon of ground ginger
- ¼ teaspoon of cinnamon
- Black pepper, to taste

DIRECTIONS

1. Mix soy sauce, cloves, ginger, cinnamon, and black pepper in a bowl and coat the strips with the mixture.
2. Arrange the strips on the grill plate.
3. Place into the top or bottom shelf of the air fryer.
4. Press the power button.
5. Turn the dial to the 'Grill' and set it to 450 °F for 15 minutes.
6. Once done, serve.

BEEF RIBS

Prep: 10 Minutes | Cooking Time: 18 Minutes | Makes: 2 Servings

INGREDIENTS

- 4 tablespoons of barbecue spice rub
- 1 tablespoon kosher salt and black pepper
- 3 tablespoons brown sugar
- 2 pounds of beef ribs (3-3 1/2 pounds), cut in thirds
- 1 cup barbecue sauce

DIRECTIONS

1. Mix salt, black pepper, brown sugar, and BBQ spice rub in a bowl.
2. Coat the ribs with oil spray and then rub them with a spice mixture.
3. Adjust the ribs on the grill plate and add them to the middle shelf of the unit.
4. Turn the dial to 'Air Fry' mode at 400°F for 18 minutes.
5. Once done, serve with BBQ sauce.

GRILLED T-BONE

Prep: 15 Minutes | Cooking Time: 12 Minutes | Makes: 2 Servings

INGREDIENTS

- 2 pounds of T-bone steaks

- Sea salt, to taste
- Black pepper, to taste
- 4 teaspoons of granulated onion
- 1 teaspoon of basil
- 1 teaspoon of red pepper flakes
- 2 tablespoons coriander
- 1 tablespoon dry mustard
- 1 tablespoon of brown sugar

DIRECTIONS

1. Mix all the seasoning in the bowl and coat the steak with it.
2. Preheat the unit by turning the dial to 'Grill' at 400°F for 10 minutes
3. Place the steaks on the grill plate and put the plate on the lower shelf
4. Let it grill for 6 minutes per side at 350°F
5. Once done serve

Poultry Recipes

Cornish Hens
Page 61

Chicken Wings
Page 62

Chicken Tenders
Page 63

Fried Chicken
Page 64

Orange Chicken
Page 66

Coconut Thai Wings
Page 69

Chicken Meat Patties
Page 70

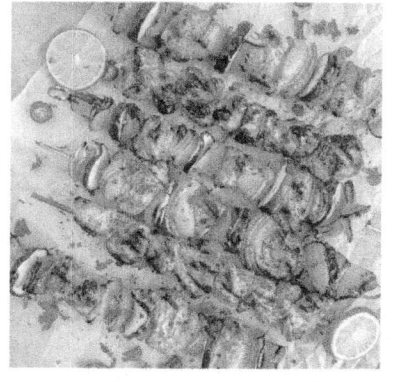
Yoghurt Lime Chicken
Page 71

Bang Chicken
Page 74

CORNISH HENS

Prep: 15 Minutes | Cooking Time: 60 Minutes | Makes: 2 Servings

INGREDIENTS

- Salt and black pepper, to taste
- 2 teaspoons garlic powder
- 2 Sprigs of rosemary
- 2 Cornish hens

DIRECTIONS

1. Rub the hens with salt, pepper, rosemary, and garlic powder.
2. Arrange the hens on the rotisserie shaft and secure the forks.
3. Tie hens with twine to keep intact.
4. Now place it inside the unit.
5. Turn the function dial to the 'Rotisserie' button and cook at 350°F for 60 minutes.
6. Once the internal temperature reaches 160 °F it's done. Take out, and serve.

ROASTED CHICKEN WITH HERBS

Prep: 15 Minutes | Cooking Time: 30 Minutes | Makes: 3 Servings

INGREDIENTS

- 1.5-pounds of chicken with skin on
- ½ tablespoons garlic powder
- 2 teaspoon onion powder
- ½ teaspoon thyme
- 2 tablespoons olive oil
- Salt and black pepper, to taste

DIRECTIONS

1. Rub the chicken with olive oil and then rub with all of the listed spices and seasoning
2. Place inside the crisper tray.
3. Turn the function dial to 'Air Fry' and cook for 30 minutes at 350°F.
4. Once the cooking time is complete, serve, and enjoy.

FRIED CHICKEN STRIPS

Prep: 12 Minutes | Cooking Time: 35 Minutes | Makes: 2 Servings

INGREDIENTS

- 350 g chicken breast cut into strips
- 4 large eggs
- 1/3 cup milk
- 50 grams flour
- 150 grams breadcrumbs
- 1 teaspoon olive oil
- Salt and black pepper, to taste

DIRECTIONS

1. Take a bowl and add breadcrumbs.
2. Then mix in the olive oil.
3. Pour the flour into a separate large bowl.

4. Whisk egg and milk in a large third bowl.
5. Dip the chicken strips in the flour, then in egg, and finally in the breadcrumb mixture.
6. Arrange the pieces onto the grill plate.
7. Turn the function dial to 'Air Fry' and adjust the timer to cook for 35 minutes at 350°F.
8. Flip the strips halfway through cooking.
9. Once golden, serve, and enjoy.

CHICKEN WINGS

Prep: 15 Minutes | Cooking Time: 40 Minutes | Makes: 2 Servings

INGREDIENTS

- 1 cup Louisiana chicken batter mix
- 10 chicken wings
- ½ teaspoon of smoked paprika
- 2 tablespoons of Dijon mustard
- 1 tablespoon of cayenne pepper
- 1 teaspoon of meat tenderizer powder
- Oil spray, for greasing

DIRECTIONS

1. Add the chicken wings, mustard, paprika, batter mix, cayenne pepper, and meat tenderizer into a bowl and coat the wings.
2. Grease lightly with oil spray.
3. Add wings to the baking pan and adjust the pan inside the unit.
4. Turn the function dial to 'Air Fry' and cook for 40 minutes at 400°F.
5. Flip wings halfway through the cooking time.
6. Serve and enjoy hot.

CHICKEN BREAST

Prep: 12 Minutes | Cooking Time: 30 Minutes | Makes: 2 Servings

INGREDIENT S

- 2 large organic eggs
- 1-ounce buttermilk
- 1 cup of cornmeal
- ¼ cup almond flour
- Salt and black pepper, to taste
- 4 chicken breasts
- 2 tablespoons of oil bay seasoning

DIRECTIONS

1. Whisk eggs with buttermilk in a large bowl.
2. In a separate medium bowl mix almond flour, cornmeal, salt, black pepper, and oil bay seasoning.
3. Dip the chicken breast into egg, and then dredge with the cornmeal mixture.
4. Coat pieces all over.
5. Layer onto the baking pan and place into the middle positions of the air fryer.
6. Turn the function dial to 'Air Fry' set it to cook for 30 minutes at 350°F.
7. Hit the 'Start' button to commence cooking.

8. Once 15 minutes have passed, take out the pan and flip the breast pieces.
9. Add them back to the unit and continue with the cooking cycle.
10. Once the cooking cycle is done, serve.

CHICKEN TENDERS

Prep: 15 Minutes | Cooking Time: 30 Minutes | Makes: 2 Servings

INGREDIENTS

- 1 cup flour
- 2 large eggs
- 2 ounces almond milk
- 1 cup Panko breadcrumbs
- 6 chicken tenders
- Salt and black pepper, to taste
- 6 ounces honey mustard, side serving

DIRECTIONS

1. Add flour to a pan.
2. Whisk egg and milk in a bowl.
3. Add breadcrumbs, salt, and black pepper to a flat tray.
4. Add each chicken tender into the flour, then in the egg wash, and then and finally in the breadcrumbs.
5. Arrange the pieces onto the baking pan.
6. Place pan in the middle shelf of the unit.
7. Turn the function dial to 'Air Fry' and cook for 30 minutes at 350°F.
8. Flip the strips halfway through cooking.
9. Once golden, serve, and enjoy with the honey mustard.

BUFFALO WINGS

Prep: 15 Minutes | Cooking Time: 40 Minutes | Makes: 2 Servings

INGREDIENTS

- 12 chicken wings
- Salt and black pepper, to taste
- 100 ml Buffalo sauce

DIRECTIONS

1. Season the chicken wings with salt, pepper, and olive oil
2. Place into the air fryer baking pan and adjust it on the middle shelf.
3. Turn the function dial to 'Air Fry' and cook for 40 minutes at 400°F.
4. Once half the time has passed, shake the pan and put it back into the oven.
5. Serve wings with the buffalo sauce.

SWEET AND SPICY CHICKEN WINGS

Prep: 10 Minutes | Cooking Time: 30 Minutes | Makes: 2 Servings

INGREDIENTS

- 1 cup ketchup
- ½ cup sugar
- 2 tablespoons hot sauce
- 5 tablespoons water

- 2 tablespoons white vinegar
- 10 chicken wings
- 1 cup ranch dressing, for serving

DIRECTIONS

1. Take a bowl and add water, ketchup, sugar, hot sauce, and white vinegar.
2. Transfer to a saucepan and simmer on a low heat.
3. Once thickened, baste the chicken with the sauce.
4. Arrange chicken onto the grill plate and place the plate on the bottom shelf.
5. Turn the function dial to 'Air Fry' and cook for 30 minutes at 400°F.
6. Once half the time has passed, flip the wings and baste with more sauce.
7. Once the wings are done, serve the wings with the remaining sauce and the ranch dressing.

FRIED CHICKEN

Prep: 20 Minutes | Cooking Time: 30 Minutes | Makes: 2 Servings

INGREDIENTS

- 3 chicken thighs
- 3 chicken legs
- 250 grams flour
- 1 tablespoon garlic powder
- 1 teaspoon onion powder
- 1 teaspoon cumin
- 1 tablespoon paprika
- Salt and black pepper, to taste
- 1 tablespoon olive oil
- 200 ml buttermilk

DIRECTIONS

1. First, soak the chicken in buttermilk for 2 hours in the refrigerator.
2. Mix flour, oil, pepper, garlic powder, onion powder, poultry seasoning, cumin, pepper, and salt in a bowl and set aside.
3. Dip chicken into flour, and then in the buttermilk, and then in the flour mixture.
4. Place inside the air fryer baking pan lined with parchment paper.
5. Turn the function dial to 'Air Fry' and cook for 30 minutes at 400°F.
6. Turn the pieces over every 10 minutes.
7. Serve once done.

HOT AND SPICY CHICKEN

Prep: 25 Minutes | Cooking Time: 40 Minutes | Makes: 3 Servings

Ingredients

- 4 chicken thighs
- 4 chicken wings
- 4 chicken breasts
- 2 cups buttermilk
- 2 cups almond flour
- Oil spray, for greasing
- 8 tablespoons of tomato sauce
- 2 teaspoons of sugar
- Salt, to taste
- 1/2 cup butter

SEASONING

- Salt and black pepper, to taste
- 1 tablespoon garlic powder
- 1 teaspoon onion powder
- 2 teaspoons cumin
- 2 tablespoons paprika
- 1 tablespoon cayenne pepper
- 1 teaspoon turmeric
- 1 teaspoon garlic powder
- 1 tablespoon salt
- 1 teaspoon sugar

DIRECTIONS

1. First, soak the chicken pieces in buttermilk for 2 hours in the refrigerator.
2. Combine all of the seasoning ingredients in a separate bowl along with the flour.
3. Take out chicken from buttermilk and dip into flour, then in buttermilk, and then in the flour mixture.
4. Arrange the chicken onto the crisper tray.
5. Lightly grease the pieces with oil spray.
6. Turn the function dial to 'Air Fry' and set it to cook for 40 minutes at 400°F at 'Air Fry' mode.
7. Mix tomato sauce, salt, pepper, and sugar along with butter in a saucepan and cook until thick.
8. Once the chicken is cooked drizzle sauce over the chicken.
9. Enjoy.

CHICKEN MILANESE

Prep: 15 Minutes | Cooking Time: 30 Minutes | Makes: 2 Servings

INGREDIENTS

- 2 cups Panko breadcrumbs
- ¼ cup parmesan
- ½ teaspoon garlic powder
- 2 eggs
- 4 chicken cutlets
- Salt and black pepper, to taste
- 2 teaspoons white wine vinegar
- 1 lemon, juice only
- 4 tablespoons extra virgin olive oil
- 2 cups arugula
- 1 beefsteak tomato, sliced
- 1/3 cup shaved parmesan cheese

DIRECTIONS

1. Mix cheese, breadcrumbs, and garlic powder in a bowl.
2. Season cutlets with salt and black pepper.
3. Dip cutlets in eggs then in the Panko mixture.
4. Arrange onto the crisper tray.
5. Turn the function dial to 'Air Fry' and top shelf of the PowerXL Air Fryer Grill.
6. Press the 'Air Fry' button and set it to cook for 30 minutes at 350 °F.
7. Flip cutlets halfway through cooking.
8. While cooking, prepare the salad by mixing vinegar, tomato, lemon juice,

and oil in a bowl and adding arugula to it.
9. Toss well and serve with the cooked chicken and a sprinkle of cheese on top.

ORANGE CHICKEN

Prep: 15 Minutes | Cooking Time: 40 Minutes | Makes: 2 Servings

INGREDIENTS

- 1 pound boneless & skinless chicken breast, cubed
- 2 eggs, beaten
- 1.5 cups cornstarch
- Salt and black pepper, to taste

SAUCE INGREDIENTS

- 4 teaspoons soy sauce
- 4 teaspoons brown sugar
- 1 teaspoon ginger, grated
- 1 teaspoon garlic, grated
- 2 teaspoons rice vinegar
- 1 tablespoon chopped scallion
- Pinch of red pepper flakes
- 1 teaspoon of orange zest
- 1 cup orange juice
- 2 tablespoons butter

DIRECTIONS

1. Preheat the air fryer.
2. Whisk eggs in a bowl and add chicken wings.
3. Mix cornstarch, salt, and pepper in a bowl.
4. Coat chicken with the cornstarch mixture then shake off the excess cornstarch.
5. Put the pieces onto the crisper tray and place them on the middle shelf
6. Turn the function dial to 'Air Fry' and cook at 400°F for 30 minutes.
7. Meanwhile, mix all of the sauce ingredients in a saucepan and bring to a boil.
8. Lower the heat to a simmer.
9. Once the chicken is cooked, toss it in the sauce and serve.

CHICKEN LEG

Prep: 12 Minutes | Cooking Time: 35 Minutes | Makes: 2 Servings

INGREDIENTS

- 2 teaspoons of onion powder
- ½ teaspoon of paprika powder
- ½ teaspoon of garlic powder
- Salt and black pepper, to taste
- 2 tablespoons of Italian seasoning
- 2 teaspoons of celery seeds
- 2 eggs, whisked
- 1/2 cup buttermilk
- 1 cup of corn flour
- 1 pound of chicken leg pieces

DIRECTIONS

1. Whisk the egg in a bowl and add buttermilk, salt, and pepper. Set aside.
2. Now in a small bowl add all of the spices and the flour.

3. Dredge chicken in egg then in the flour mixture.
4. Lightly coat the chicken legs with oil spray.
5. Put the leg pieces into the air fryer crisper tray.
6. Turn the function dial to 'Air Fry' and set it to 360°F for 40 minutes.
7. Once done, serve, and enjoy.

EASY CHICKEN BREASTS

Prep: 15 Minutes | Cooking Time: 30 Minutes | Makes: 2 Servings

INGREDIENTS

- 4 large chicken breasts, 6 ounces each
- 2 tablespoons of Old Bay seasoning
- 1 tablespoon Montreal chicken seasoning
- 1 teaspoon of thyme
- 1/2 teaspoon of paprika
- Salt, to taste
- Oil spray, for greasing

DIRECTIONS

1. Season the chicken breasts with the old bay seasoning, thyme, Montreal seasoning, paprika, and salt.
2. Lightly grease with oil spray and add to the crisper tray.
3. Place the trays on the middle shelf of the PowerXL Air Fryer Grill.
4. Turn the function dial to 'Air Fry' and set it to cook at 350°F for 30 minutes.
5. After 15 minutes of cooking flip the breasts over.
6. Then continue with the remaining cooking time.
7. Once the chicken is cooked, serve.

SPICY CHICKEN BREAST

Prep: 15 Minutes | Cooking Time: 35 Minutes | Makes: 2 Servings

INGREDIENTS

- 4 chicken breasts
- 1 cup buttermilk
- 1.5 cups of almond flour
- Salt and black pepper, to taste
- 2 tablespoons of Italian seasoning
- Oil spray, for greasing

DIRECTIONS

1. Pour buttermilk into a bowl and soak the breast in it for 1 hour.
2. Mix flour with Italian seasoning, salt, and black pepper in a bowl.
3. Dip the chicken into the almond flour.
4. Then coat with the buttermilk and then with the flour mixture.
5. Arrange the chicken onto the crisper tray which is lightly greased with oil spray.
6. Place the tray onto the middle of the PowerXL Air Fryer Grill.

7. Turn the function dial to 'Grill' and cook for 35 minutes at 360°F.
8. Flip the chicken halfway through cooking.
9. Once done, serve.

SPICY CURRIED CHICKEN WINGS RECIPE

Prep: 15 Minutes | Cooking Time: 35 Minutes | Makes: 2 Servings

INGREDIENTS

- 1/4 tablespoons red chilli powder
- 1/4 tablespoons curry powder
- Sea salt, to taste
- Pinch of white pepper
- 1/3 teaspoon of minced garlic
- 10 chicken wings
- 2-3 tablespoons of olive oil

DIRECTIONS

1. Place the chicken wings in a large mixing bowl and add the red chilli powder, curry powder, salt, garlic, and white pepper.
2. Add olive oil and coat the chicken well with the spice rub.
3. Put in refrigerator for 1 hour.
4. Now place the wings on the crisper tray.
5. Place the tray on the top, middle, or bottom shelf.
6. Turn the function dial to 'Air Fry' and set the timer for 35 minutes at 360°F.

7. Once 15 minutes have passed, take out the tray and flip the wings.
8. Cook for the remaining time.
9. The internal temperature of the chicken should reach 165.
10. Serve the chicken and enjoy.

CHICKEN WINGS WITH SESAME AND SOY

Prep: 15 Minutes | Cooking Time: 40 minutes | Makes: 5 Servings

INGREDIENTS

- 4 tablespoons of sesame seeds
- 2 tablespoons of olive oil
- 5 tablespoons of honey
- 2 tablespoons soy sauce
- 1 tablespoon of ginger-garlic paste
- 10 chicken drumsticks

DIRECTIONS

1. Add sesame seeds, olive oil, honey, soy sauce, and ginger-garlic paste to a bowl and mix well.
2. Coat the chicken drumsticks with the marinade.
3. Place the drumsticks on the crisper tray.
4. Put the crisper tray inside the PowerXL Air Fryer Grill in either the top or middle position.
5. Turn the function dial to 'Air Fry' and cook for 40 minutes at 370°F.
6. Halfway through the cooking time, flip the chicken drumsticks.
7. Cook at 370 for the remaining time.

8. Serve.

GLAZED THIGHS

Prep: 15 Minutes | Cooking Time: 30 Minutes | Makes: 2 Servings

INGREDIENTS

- 2 tablespoons of soy sauce
- Salt and black pepper, to taste
- 1 teaspoon of Worcestershire Sauce
- 2 teaspoons brown sugar
- 1 teaspoon of garlic, paste
- 6 boneless chicken thighs
- 1 pound of hand-cut potato fries (thick)
- 2 tablespoons of canola oil
- ½ cup ranch dressing, side serving

DIRECTIONS

1. Take a bowl and mix the soy sauce, Worcestershire sauce, brown sugar, and garlic paste.
2. Put the thighs into the marinade and let sit for 40 minutes in the refrigerator.
3. Meanwhile, coat the potatoes with canola oil and season them with salt and black pepper.
4. Now place the potatoes and chicken onto the crisper tray and place them on the top shelf.
5. Turn the function dial to 'Air Fry' and cook at 400°F for 30 minutes.
6. After 10 minutes, take out the tray and flip the things and turn the potato wedges.
7. Now place back inside the oven and continue to cook for 10 minutes.
8. Serve with ranch dressing.

COCONUT THAI WINGS

Prep: 12 Minutes | Cooking Time: 40 Minutes | Makes: 3 Servings

INGREDIENTS

- 12 chicken wings, skinless
- 16 ounces of full-fat coconut milk
- 1/3 cup reduced-sodium soy sauce
- 1/3 cup rice vinegar
- 1 red Thai chilli pepper, sliced
- 2 tablespoons of sunflower oil
- 1 tablespoon brown sugar
- 1 teaspoon natural peanut butter
- 4 cloves of garlic, minced

DIRECTIONS

1. In a plastic zip lock bag place the coconut milk, minced garlic, soy sauce, rice vinegar, chilli pepper, sunflower oil, brown sugar, and butter.
2. Marinate the wings in this mixture for 2 hours in the refrigerator.
3. Afterwards, take out the chicken from the marinade and place it inside an oil-greased baking pan.
4. Place the baking pan inside the air fryer.

5. Turn the function dial to 'Air Fry' and adjust the temperature to cook at 400°F.
6. The chicken will be fully cooked once the internal temperature reaches 165 °F.
7. Take out of the baking pan and serve the chicken.

ROASTED CHICKEN WITH APPLE

Prep: 10 Minutes | Cooking Time: 110 Minutes | Makes: 2 Servings

INGREDIENTS

- 2 gala apples, peeled and round sliced
- 4 tablespoons unsalted butter
- 1 tablespoon orange zest
- 1 teaspoon cinnamon
- 1 pound of whole chicken, pieces or cut them in half
- Salt, to taste
- 1 teaspoon of garlic paste
- Oil spray, for greasing

DIRECTIONS

1. Grease a baking pan with oil spray and set aside.
2. Mix butter, cinnamon, orange zest, garlic, salt in a bowl and rub the chicken with the mixture.
3. Now arrange the apple slices on the bottom of the baking pan and place the coated chicken pieces on top.
4. Lightly coat the chicken with oil spray.

5. Turn the dial on the air fryer by pressing the 'Chicken' button and adjust the time to cook for 110 minutes at 370°F.
6. Serve hot with caramelized apple slices from the bottom on top of the cooked chicken.
7. Enjoy!

CHICKEN MEAT PATTIES

Prep: 10 minutes | Cooking Time: 35 minutes | Makes: 4 Servings

INGREDIENTS

- 2 pounds of chicken, cooked and shredded
- Ground black pepper, to taste
- Salt, to taste
- 1 egg
- 1 shallot
- 2 potatoes, boiled and mashed
- 1 green chilli, chopped
- ½ teaspoon coriander powder
- ½ teaspoon of turmeric
- Ketchup, side serving
- 1 cup Panko breadcrumbs
- Oil spray for greasing

DIRECTIONS

1. Take a mixing bowl and add ground meat, shallots, salt, pepper, egg, mashed potato, green chilli, coriander, and turmeric.
2. Mix well and make patties of the meat mixture.

3. Coat the patties well with the Panko breadcrumbs.
4. Lightly coat the patties with oil spray.
5. Arrange the patties onto the oil-greased crisper tray.
6. Put the tray on the top or middle shelf.
7. Press the 'Power' button and cook for 35 minutes at 300°F.
8. Flip the patties halfway through the cooking period.
9. Once done, serve with the ketchup.
10. Enjoy.

SESAME FLAVORED CHICKEN BREAST

Prep: 15 Minutes | Cooking Time: 30 Minutes | Makes: 4 Servings

INGREDIENTS

- 2 tablespoons of sesame seeds
- 4 tablespoons of sesame oil
- 2 tablespoons of coconut sugar
- 2 tablespoons coconut amino
- Salt, pinch
- 2 tablespoons of lemon juice
- 2 pounds of chicken breasts

DIRECTIONS

1. Mix sesame seeds, sesame oil, coconut sugar, coconut amino, salt, and lemon juice in a bowl and add chicken breast pieces.
2. Coat pieces well and marinate for a few hours in the refrigerator.
3. Add the chicken to the grill plate.
4. Place the plates on the middle shelf of the PowerXL Air Fryer Grill.
5. Turn the function dial to 'Air Fry' and set the timer for 30 minutes at 370°F.
6. After 15 minutes flip the chicken.
7. Once the cooking time is complete, serve.

YOGURT LIME CHICKEN

Prep: 10 Minutes | Cooking Time: 40 Minutes | Makes: 2 Servings

INGREDIENTS

- 2 pounds chicken breasts, boneless and skinless
- 4 cloves of garlic, minced
- 1 lime, zest, and juice
- 2 tablespoons canola oil
- 1 cup plain yogurt
- Salt and black pepper, to taste
- ¼ teaspoon of red chilli powder
- Pinch of turmeric powder
- 1 teaspoon of Garam Masala powder

DIRECTIONS

1. Mix yogurt with Garam Masala powder, red chilli powder, salt, pepper, canola oil, lime zest, and juice, and minced garlic.
2. Mix well and marinate the chicken for 2 hours in the refrigerator.
3. Now put the chicken into a greased baking pan and place the pan inside the air fryer.

4. Turn the function dial to 'Air Fry' and cook for 40 minutes at 400°F.
5. Once done, serve.

PARMESAN BREADED FRIED CHICKEN TENDERS

Prep: 12 Minutes | Cooking Time: 30 Minutes | Makes: 4 Servings

INGREDIENTS

- 2 pounds skinless chicken breast, cut into strips
- 1 cup parmesan cheese, freshly grated
- 1/2 cup Panko breadcrumbs
- 2 eggs
- 2 teaspoons Italian Seasoning
- Salt and pepper to taste
- Oil spray, for greasing

DIRECTIONS

1. Whisk eggs in a bowl and set aside.
2. In a flat tray mix breadcrumbs, Italian seasoning, salt, pepper, and Parmesan cheese.
3. Now dip the chicken strips into the egg and then coat with the parmesan crumb mixture.
4. Repeat for all chicken strips.
5. Now arrange the chicken strips on the crisper tray.
6. Place the tray on the top shelf.
7. Turn the function dial to 'Air Fry' and adjust the time to 30 minutes at 350°F.
8. Once strips get crispy, serve immediately.

PINEAPPLE CHICKEN

Prep: 20 Minutes | Cooking Time: 35 Minutes | Makes: 2 Servings

INGREDIENTS

MARINADE

- 1 cup of pineapple juice
- 4 tablespoons of ketchup
- 1/2 cup of soy sauce
- 1 tablespoon of dark brown sugar
- 4 cloves of garlic, minced
- 1-inch ginger, grated

OTHER INGREDIENTS

- 4 large boneless skinless chicken breasts
- 1 pineapple, sliced into rings
- Oil spray, for greasing

DIRECTIONS

1. Grease the pineapple slices with oil spray.
2. Mix all of the marinade ingredients in a bowl.
3. Whisk well until the sugar dissolves.
4. Pour this marinade into a plastic zip-lock bag and add chicken.
5. Refrigerate for 2 hours.
6. Afterwards, arrange the marinated chicken pieces inside the baking pan.

7. Put the baking pan inside the air fryer.
8. Adjust the timer to 400 °F for 30 minutes by pressing the Chicken button.
9. After 30 minutes take out the baking pan and add the oil-greased pineapple slices to the baking pan on top of the chicken.
10. Cook for 5 more minutes at 400 °F.
11. Slice chicken and serve with the pineapple slices.

BALSAMIC VINEGAR CHICKEN BREASTS

Prep: 12 Minutes | Cooking Time: 30 Minutes | Makes: 5 Servings

INGREDIENTS

- 2 tablespoons of coconut oil
- 5 tablespoons balsamic vinegar
- 2 cloves of garlic, minced
- 1/3 teaspoon of red chilli powder
- Salt and black pepper, to taste
- 10 chicken breasts, boneless and skinless

DIRECTIONS

1. Mix coconut oil, balsamic vinegar, garlic, salt, black pepper, and chilli powder in a large bowl.
2. Coat the chicken in the mixture.
3. Marinate for 1 hour.
4. Now arrange the chicken strips on the crisper tray of the PowerXL Air Fryer Grill.
5. Place the trays on the top shelf.
6. Turn the function dial to 'Air Fry' and set it to cook for 30 minutes at 350°F.
7. Once the chicken's internal temperature reaches 165 °F serve.

SRIRACHA-HONEY WINGS

Prep: 10 Minutes | Cooking Time: 30 Minutes | Makes: 2 Servings

INGREDIENTS

- 8 chicken wings
- 1/4 cup honey
- 4 tablespoons of Sriracha sauce
- 2 tablespoons of soy sauce
- 2 tablespoons of butter
- Salt and black pepper, to taste
- 1 teaspoon of lemon juice
- ½ cup cilantro, for garnishing
- Oil spray, for greasing

DIRECTIONS

1. Coat the chicken with oil spray, and season with salt and black pepper.
2. Now arrange the chicken wings on the crisper tray.
3. Place the tray on the top shelf of the PowerXL Air Fryer Grill.
4. Flip the wings halfway through the cooking time.
5. Meanwhile, in a saucepan melt butter and add honey, Sriracha sauce, soy sauce, and lemon juice.

6. Turn dial function to the 'Air Fry' mode button and cook for 30 minutes at 350°F.
7. When cooked, the internal temperature should reach 165 degrees.
8. Once the chicken is cooked, toss the wings in the sauce and serve with a garnish of cilantro.

BANG CHICKEN

Prep: 15 Minutes | Cooking Time: 30 Minutes | Makes: 2 Servings

INGREDIENTS

CHICKEN SAUCE

- 1/3 cup mayonnaise
- 2 tablespoons of raw honey
- 1/3 tablespoon Sriracha sauce or to taste

CHICKEN BATTER INGREDIENTS

- 1 cup buttermilk
- 1/4 cup all-purpose flour (or more if needed)
- 1/2 cup cornstarch
- 2 eggs, whisked
- 2 teaspoons Sriracha sauce or to taste
- Salt and black pepper to taste
- Other ingredients
- 1 pound of chicken breast cut them in half
- 1.5 cups Panko breadcrumbs
- Oil spray, for greasing

DIRECTIONS

1. Mix all of the sauce ingredients in a large mixing bowl and set aside.
2. Combine buttermilk, corn starch, flour, eggs, Sriracha, salt, and pepper.
3. Dip chicken pieces into buttermilk batter and then into the breadcrumbs.
4. Repeat until all pieces are well coated.
5. Arrange the pieces on a baking pan.
6. Put inside the PowerXL Air Fryer Grill.
7. Turn the function dial to 'Air Fry' and cook for 30 minutes at 360°F.
8. Once done, serve.

CHIPOTLE CHICKEN WINGS

Prep: 15 Minutes | Cooking Time: 30 Minutes | Makes: 2 Servings

INGREDIENTS

- 1 teaspoon chilli powder
- 1 teaspoon ground cumin
- 4 boneless chicken breasts
- 2 teaspoons chipotle flakes
- 1 teaspoon Mexican oregano
- Salt and ground black pepper to taste
- ½ lime, juiced

DIRECTIONS

1. Mix all of the spices in a bowl and combine well.
2. Rub the chicken breast pieces with the spice rub.

3. Lightly grease the breasts with some oil spray.
4. Place the breasts on the crisper tray and arrange the tray on the middle shelf.
5. Turn the function dial to 'Air Fry' and cook for 30 minutes at 350°F.
6. Once done, serve.

GINGER CHICKEN

Prep: 15 Minutes | Cooking Time: 30 Minutes | Makes: 2 Servings

INGREDIENTS

- 1 pound chicken wings, disjointed and with tips
- ½ cup of soy sauce
- 2 tablespoons of brown sugar
- 2 tablespoons of ginger root, minced
- 4 cloves of garlic, minced
- Oil spray, for greasing
- 1 tablespoon of five-spice powders

DIRECTIONS

1. Combine brown sugar, soy sauce, ginger, garlic, and five-spice powder.
2. Rub over the chicken and let marinate in the refrigerator for a few hours.
3. Next, take the crisper tray and grease them with oil spray.
4. Put the chicken onto the crisper tray.
5. Place inside the air fryer on the top shelf.
6. Turn the function dial to 'Air Fry' and set the timer to 30 minutes at 350°F.
7. Flip halfway through the cooking time.
8. Serve.

BBQ WINGS

Prep: 15 Minutes | Cooking Time: 45 Minutes | Makes: 2 Servings

INGREDIENTS

- 1 pound of chicken wings
- 1/3 cup BBQ sauce

DIRECTIONS

1. Place the wing on the crisper tray of the air fryer.
2. Put it on the lower shelf.
3. Turn on the function dial to 'Air Fry' at 400°F for 45 minutes.
4. Turn wings halfway through.
5. Once it's cooked toss in BBQ sauce and serve.

CHICKEN TOMATINA

Prep: 15 Minutes | Cooking Time: 30 Minutes | Makes: 2 Servings

INGREDIENTS

- 2 chicken breasts, boneless and skinless
- 1/8 cup fresh basil leaves
- 6 plum tomatoes
- 1/4 cup lemon juice

- 2 tablespoons olive oil
- ½ garlic clove, minced
- ½ inch of ginger, chopped
- Salt and black pepper, to taste

DIRECTIONS

1. Use a food processor to blend all the listed ingredients except chicken.
2. Once smooth take it out and marinate chicken in it for 1 hour.
3. Then put the chicken onto the baking pan and place the pan on the lower shelf.
4. Turn the dial to 'Air Fry' at 390°F for 30 minutes.
5. Once done, serve.

MAPLE CHICKEN WING

Prep: 15 Minutes | Cooking Time: 30 Minutes | Makes: 4 Servings

INGREDIENTS

- Salt, to taste
- 1/4 teaspoon smoked paprika
- 1.5 pounds chicken wings, rinsed, patted dry
- ½ tablespoon garlic, minced
- ½ tablespoon lemon juice
- ½ teaspoon crushed red pepper
- ½ tablespoon fresh rosemary, chopped
- ½ cup Maple syrup

DIRECTIONS

1. First, put grill plate inside the unit and turn dial function to 'Air Fry' at 400°F for 10 minutes
2. Let it preheat for 10 minutes
3. Meanwhile, coat wings with salt, garlic, and smoked paprika.
4. Turn the dial to 'Air Fry' for 30 minutes at 400°F.
5. Transfer the chicken wings to a baking pan and put the pan on the lower shelf.
6. Let it air fry at 400°F for 25-30 minutes.
7. Meanwhile, combine lemon juice, rosemary, red pepper, and maple syrup.
8. Remember to flip it halfway through.
9. Once the wings are ready, transfer to the sauce bowl to coat the wings.
10. Serve.

Rotisserie Recipes

Apple Maple Glazed Ham
Page 81

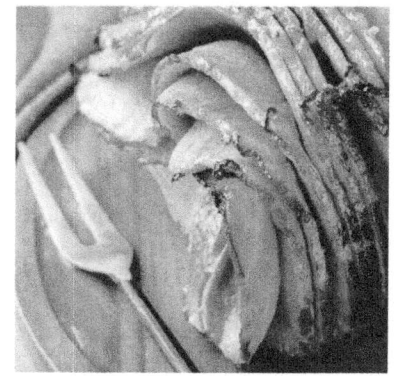
Sugared Glazed Ham
Page 82

Smoked Dijon Ham
Page 85

Cornish Hens
Page 87

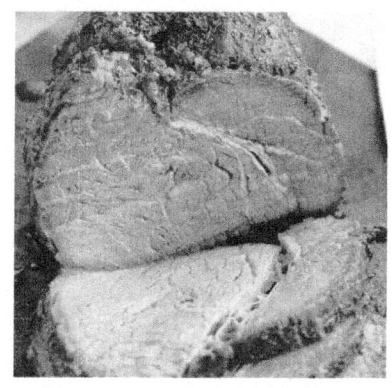
Rotisserie Beef Chuck
Page 90

Marinated Beef Roast
Page 92

Aleppo Prime Rib
Page 93

Mediterranean Lamb
Page 95

Marinade Lamb Leg
Page 96

APPLE MAPLE GLAZED HAM

Prep: 10 Minutes | Cooking Time: 30 Minutes | Makes: 2 Servings

INGREDIENTS

- 1.5-pound ham
- 1/2 cup apple juice
- 4 tablespoons maple syrup
- Pinch of cinnamon, powder
- Salt, pinch

DIRECTIONS

1. Combine apple juice with a pinch of salt, maple syrup, and cinnamon.
2. Whisk the ingredients well.
3. Now coat the ham with the bowl mixture and set aside for a while
4. Add one of the forks to the spit and tighten the screws on the fork. Slide the ham onto the spit and into the secured fork. Secure the ham on the spit and insert the spit into the rotisserie connections.
5. Turn the function dial to 'Rotisserie' and set the timer to 30 minutes at 350°F.
6. After every 5 minutes brush the ham with the bowl mixture.
7. Once cooked, remove and serve once slightly cooled down.

PINEAPPLE GLAZED HAM

Prep: 10 Minutes | Cooking Time: 30 Minutes | Makes: 2 Servings

INGREDIENTS

- 2 pounds of ham
- 1 cup pineapple, chunks
- 4 cans pineapple juice
- ¼ cup brown sugar

DIRECTIONS

1. Preheat the air fryer to 350 °F.
2. Place the ham into a roasting pan and rub with the brown sugar.
3. Pin the pineapple slices onto the ham using toothpicks.
4. Add one of the forks to the spit and tighten the screws on the fork. Slide the ham onto the spit and into the secured fork. Secure the ham on the spit and insert the spit into the rotisserie connections.
5. Turn the function dial to 'Rotisserie' and set the timer to 30 minutes at 350°F.
6. After every 5 minutes, brush the ham with pineapple juice.
7. Once done, remove and serve once slightly cooled.

ORANGE GLAZE HAM

Prep: 10 Minutes | Cooking Time: 35 Minutes | Makes: 2 Servings

INGREDIENTS

- 2-3 pounds of the leg of ham, bone-in, skin on
- 10 cloves

- 2 oranges, juiced
- 1/3 cup maple syrup
- Pinch of sea salt

DIRECTIONS

1. Take a bowl and mix the maple syrup, orange juice, sea salt, and cloves.
2. Simmer in a saucepan until thickened, for about 5 minutes.
3. Coat the ham with the glaze.
4. Add one of the forks to the spit and tighten the screws on the fork. Slide the ham onto the spit and into the secured fork. Secure the ham on the spit and insert the spit into the rotisserie connections.
5. Turn the function dial to 'Rotisserie' and set the timer to 30 minutes at 350°F.
6. After every 5 minutes brush the ham with the saucepan mixture.
7. Once done, remove and serve once slightly cooled.

SUGARED GLAZED HAM

Prep: 10 Minutes | Cooking Time: 30 Minutes | Makes: 2 Servings

INGREDIENTS

- 2 pounds of boneless ham
- 4 tablespoons of brown sugar
- 4 tablespoons of olive oil
- 1 tablespoon of parsley

DIRECTIONS

1. Coat the ham with olive oil.
2. Rub the ham with brown sugar and parsley.
3. Add one of the forks to the spit and tighten the screws on the fork. Slide the ham onto the spit and into the secured fork. Secure the ham on the spit and insert the spit into the rotisserie connections.
4. Turn the function dial to 'Rotisserie' and set the timer to cook for 30 minutes at 350°F.
5. Once done, remove and serve once slightly cooled.

HONEY AND CLOVE HAM

Prep: 15 Minutes | Cooking Time: 30 Minutes | Makes: 3 Servings

INGREDIENTS

- 1/3 cup honey
- 1/3 cup brown sweetener (Brown sugar can be used if preferred).
- 1/3 teaspoon ground cloves
- 2 pounds cooked ham, smoked ham

DIRECTIONS

1. In a medium bowl mix honey with brown sugar, ground cloves, and rub all over the ham.
2. Add one of the forks to the spit and tighten the screws on the fork. Slide the ham onto the spit and into the secured fork. Secure the ham on

the spit and insert the spit into the rotisserie connections.
3. Turn the function dial to 'Rotisserie' and set the timer to 30 minutes at 350°F.
4. Once done, remove and serve once slightly cooled down.

RUM GLAZED HAM

Prep: 10 Minutes | Cooking Time: 30 Minutes | Makes: 4 Servings

INGREDIENTS

- 2 pounds cooked boneless ham

GLAZE INGREDIENTS

- ½ cup dark brown sugar
- 4 tablespoons Dijon mustard
- 3 tablespoons melted butter
- ¼ teaspoon ground cloves
- 1/3 teaspoon garlic powder
- 2 teaspoons soy sauce
- ½ cup dark rum

DIRECTIONS

1. Take a bowl and combine all of the glaze ingredients in a bowl and whisk well.
2. Coat the ham with the glaze and let it sit for 30 minutes.
3. Add one of the forks to the spit and tighten the screws on the fork. Slide the ham onto the spit and into the secured fork. Secure the ham on the spit and insert the spit into the rotisserie connections.

4. Turn the function dial to 'Rotisserie' and set the timer to 30 minutes at 370°F.
5. Remember to brush the ham with the glaze every 6 minutes.
6. Once done, remove and serve once slightly cooled down.

SWEET AND SPICY GLAZED HAM

Prep: 10 Minutes | Cooking Time: 22 Minutes | Makes: 2 Servings

INGREDIENTS

- 1.5-pounds of boneless spiral ham

GLAZE INGREDIENTS

- 1 cup honey
- 1/6 cup brown sugar
- 4tablespoons Dijon mustard
- 1/3 teaspoon nutmeg
- 1/3 teaspoon cayenne pepper
- Pinch of salt

DIRECTIONS

1. In a large bowl mix all of the glaze ingredients.
2. Coat the ham with the glaze and let it sit for 30 minutes.
3. Add one of the forks to the spit and tighten the screws on the fork. Slide the ham onto the spit and into the secured fork. Secure the ham on the spit and insert the spit into the rotisserie connections.

4. Turn the function dial to 'Rotisserie' and set the timer to 30 minutes at 370°F.
5. Remember to brush the ham with the bowl glaze every 5 minutes.
6. Once done, remove and serve once slightly cooled down.

ZESTY GLAZED HAM

Prep: 10 Minutes | Cooking Time: 30 Minutes | Makes: 2 Servings

INGREDIENTS

- 2 pounds of ham

INGREDIENTS FOR SUGAR GLAZE

- 1/4 cup brown sugar
- 1/2 cup honey
- 1/3 cup lemon juice
- Salt and black pepper, to taste

DIRECTIONS

1. Combine lemon juice, honey, salt, sugar, and black pepper in a bowl and mix well until the sugar dissolves.
2. Now coat the ham with the bowl mixture and set aside for 30 minutes.
3. Add one of the forks to the spit and tighten the screws on the fork. Slide the ham onto the spit and into the secured fork. Secure the ham on the spit and insert the spit into the rotisserie connections.

4. Turn the function dial to 'Rotisserie' and set the timer to 30 minutes at 370°F.
5. After every 5 minutes brush the ham with the bowl mixture.
6. Once done, remove and serve once slightly cooled down.

BBQ GLAZED HAM

Prep: 10 Minutes | Cooking Time: 22 Minutes | Makes: 2 Servings

INGREDIENTS

- 1 pound of ham
- 3 tablespoons of barbecue rub
- Barbecue sauce and mustard, as needed

DIRECTIONS

1. Rub the ham with the BBQ rub and let it marinate for 2 hours in the refrigerator.
2. Add one of the forks to the spit and tighten the screws on the fork. Slide the ham onto the spit and into the secured fork. Secure the ham on the spit and insert the spit into the rotisserie connections.
3. Turn the function dial to 'Rotisserie' and set the timer to 30 minutes at 350°F.
4. After every 5 minutes brush the ham with the BBQ sauce and mustard.
5. Once done, remove and let it cooled.
6. Serve with additional barbecue sauce and mustard.

BOURBON HAM

Prep: 10 Minutes | Cooking Time: 25 Minutes | Makes: 2 Servings

INGREDIENTS

- 1 pound of ham

INGREDIENTS FOR GLAZE

- 1/2 cup honey
- 1/3 cup bourbon
- 3 tablespoons Dijon mustard

DIRECTIONS

1. Mix the glaze ingredients in a bowl and whisk well.
2. Coat the ham with the glaze and let it marinate for 2 hours in a refrigerator.
8. Take out the ham and add one of the forks to the spit and tighten the screws on the fork. Slide the ham onto the spit and into the secured fork. Secure the ham on the spit and insert the spit into the rotisserie connections.
3. Turn the function dial to 'Rotisserie' and set the timer to 30 minutes at 350°F.
4. After every 5 minutes brush the ham with the leftover bowl mixture.
5. Once done, remove and serve.

SMOKED DIJON HAM

Prep: 10 Minutes | Cooking Time: 28 Minutes | Makes: 2 Servings

INGREDIENTS

- 1.5-pound boneless smoked ham
- 2 tablespoons of Dijon mustard
- 1/2 cup pineapple juice
- 1/2 cup brown sugar
- 1/3 cup bourbon

DIRECTIONS

1. Place the ham onto the rotisserie and secure the ends.
2. Take a bowl and mix Dijon mustard, pineapple juice, brown sugar, and bourbon.
3. Brush it on all sides of the ham.
4. Slide the ham onto the spit and into the secured fork. Secure the ham on the spit and insert the spit into the rotisserie connections.
5. Turn the function dial to 'Rotisserie' and set the timer to 28 minutes at 350°F.
6. After every 8 minutes brush ham with the remaining glaze.
7. Once done, carefully remove from the air fryer.
8. Rest for 15 minutes before slicing and serving.

CANE SYRUP GLAZED HAM

Prep: 10 Minutes | Cooking Time: 30 Minutes | Makes: 2 Servings

INGREDIENTS

- 1.5-pounds of ham
- 10 cloves

GLAZE INGREDIENTS

- 1 cup cane syrup
- 1 teaspoon of clove, grounded
- ½ cup Dijon mustard
- 1 cup white wine, dry
- Salt and black pepper, to taste

DIRECTIONS

1. Use a sharp knife to make slits in the ham. Add cloves to the slits.
2. Then mix all of the glaze ingredients in a large bowl. Whisk until finely combined.
3. Coat the ham with the prepared glaze.
4. Slide the ham onto the spit and into the secured fork. Secure the ham on the spit and insert the spit into the rotisserie connections.
5. Turn the function dial to 'Rotisserie' and set the timer to 30 minutes at 350°F.
6. After every 5 minutes brush the ham with the bowl mixture.
7. Once done, remove and serve once slightly cooled.

CHIPOTLE GLAZED HAM

Prep: 10 Minutes | Cooking Time: 25 Minutes | Makes: 2 Servings

INGREDIENTS

- 3-pound spiral ham
- 3 ounces dark brown sugar
- ¼ cup yellow mustard
- 1 chipotles in adobo, minced
- 3/4 cups chicken broth
- Salt and pepper to taste

DIRECTIONS

1. Take a saucepan and add dark brown sugar, yellow mustard, adobo sauce, broth, salt, and pepper.
2. Cook for 10 minutes.
3. Let it sit for a while then coat the ham with the glaze.
4. Slide the ham onto the spit and into the secured fork. Secure the ham on the spit and insert the spit into the rotisserie connections.
5. Turn the function dial to 'Rotisserie' and set the timer to 30 minutes at 350°F.
6. Once done, remove and serve once slightly cooled.

CHELSEA GOLDEN SYRUP

Prep: 10 Minutes | Cooking Time: 30 Minutes | Makes: 2 Servings

INGREDIENTS

- 4 tablespoons of orange marmalade
- 5 whole cloves
- 1/2 cup Chelsea Golden Syrup
- 1 tablespoon of Dijon mustard
- 2-pound spiral ham

DIRECTIONS

1. Take a bowl and combine the orange marmalade, cloves, golden syrup, and Dijon mustard.
2. Glaze the ham with the mixture and let it sit for 30 minutes.
3. Slide the ham onto the spit and into the secured fork. Secure the ham on the spit and insert the spit into the rotisserie connections.
4. Turn the function dial to 'Rotisserie' and set the timer to 30 minutes at 350°F.
5. Once done, remove and serve once slightly cooled.

MUSTARD AND PLUM GLAZED HAM

Prep: 10 Minutes | Cooking Time: 40 Minutes | Makes: 2 Servings

INGREDIENTS

- 2-3 pounds of ham
- 4 tablespoons of plum jam
- 6 tablespoons of pomegranate juice
- 1/8 teaspoon of ground cloves
- 1 teaspoon of Dijon mustard

DIRECTIONS

1. Take a saucepan and add plum jam, pomegranate juice, Dijon mustard, and ground cloves.
2. Cook for 3 minutes. Let it sit for a while.
3. Coat the ham with the glaze.
4. Slide the ham onto the spit and into the secured fork. Secure the ham on the spit and insert the spit into the rotisserie connections.
5. Turn the function dial to 'Rotisserie' and set the timer to 35 minutes at 350°F.
6. Once done, remove and serve once slightly cooled.

CORNISH HENS

Prep: 15 Minutes | Cooking Time: 60 Minutes | Makes: 2 Servings

INGREDIENTS

- Salt, to taste
- 1 teaspoon of paprika powder
- 2 teaspoons thyme
- 2 tablespoons of olive oil
- 2 springs of rosemary
- 1.5-pounds of Cornish hen

DIRECTIONS

1. Rub the hens with salt, paprika, olive oil, thyme, and rosemary.
2. Slide the hen onto the spit and into the secured fork. Secure the hen on the spit and insert the spit into the rotisserie connections.
3. Now place it inside the Power XL Air Fryer grill.
4. Turn the function dial to 'Rotisserie' and cook for 60 minutes at 350°F.
5. Once the internal temperature reaches 160 °F the hen is cooked
6. Take out and let it sit for a few minutes before serving.

BUTTERMILK MARINATED HEN

Prep: 10 Minutes | Cooking Time: 40 Minutes | Makes: 2 Servings

INGREDIENTS

- 2-pound hen, whole
- Kosher salt, to taste
- 1-pint buttermilk
- 2 tablespoons of poultry seasoning

DIRECTIONS

1. First, season the hen with salt and then place it in a large bowl.
2. Pour in the buttermilk, enough to cover the chicken.
3. Place inside refrigerator for 5 hours or even overnight.
4. Now when you want to prepare chicken press the 'Power' button of the air fryer and set it to 400 °F for 5 minutes.
5. Meanwhile, remove the chicken from the buttermilk mixture.
6. Shake the hen to drain off the excess buttermilk.
7. Season the chicken with salt and poultry seasoning.
8. Slide the chicken onto the spit and into the secured fork. Secure the chicken on the spit and insert the spit into the rotisserie connections.
9. Turn the function dial to 'Rotisserie' and increase the time to 40 minutes at 350°F.
10. Once the internal temperature reaches 160°F the hen is cooked.
11. Take out and let it sit for a few minutes before serving.

SPICED CHICKEN

Prep: 10 Minutes | Cooking Time: 40 Minutes | Makes: 2 Servings

INGREDIENTS

- 2 pounds of Cornish hen

SPICE RUB INGREDIENTS

- 1/3 teaspoon garlic powder
- 1/3 teaspoon onion powder
- 1/3 teaspoon paprika
- 1/3 teaspoon lavender
- 1/3 teaspoon basil
- 1/2 teaspoon dried rosemary
- 1/3 teaspoon dried oregano
- 1/6 teaspoon dried savory
- 1/6 teaspoon dried thyme
- 1 bay leaf, crumbled
- 1/6 teaspoon coriander
- 1/6 teaspoon ground cloves

DIRECTIONS

1. Combine all of the spice rub ingredients and rub all over the chicken.
2. Arrange the chicken on the Rotisserie shaft of the air fryer.
3. Secure the forks and secure the legs of the chicken with twine.
4. Now place it inside the Power XL Air Fryer grill.
5. Turn the function dial to 'Rotisserie' and set it to 40 minutes at 370°F.
6. Once the internal temperature reaches 160 °F the chicken is cooked.
7. Take out and let it sit for a few minutes before serving.

SEASONED HEN

Prep: 10 Minutes | Cooking Time: 40 Minutes | Makes: 2 Servings

INGREDIENTS

- 1-2 pounds of whole chicken, cleaned and dry
- 4 tablespoons of ghee
- 2 tablespoons of TOG house seasoning
- Salt and black pepper, to taste

DIRECTIONS

1. Rub the chicken with salt, pepper, ghee, and TOG house seasoning.
2. Arrange the chicken on the Rotisserie shaft of the air fryer.
3. Secure the forks and tie the legs of the chicken with twine.
4. Now place it inside the Power XL Air Fryer Pro.
5. Turn the function dial to 'Rotisserie' and increase the time to 40 minutes at 400°F.
6. Once the internal temperature reaches 160 °F the chicken is cooked.
7. Take it out and let it sit for a few hours before serving.

BBQ CHICKEN

Prep: 10 Minutes | Cooking Time: 50 Minutes | Makes: 2 Servings

INGREDIENTS

- 4 tablespoons of butter
- 15 pounds of chicken
- 2 tablespoons of Trader Joe's BBQ rub and seasoning
- ½ teaspoon garlic powder
- 1/4 teaspoon of onion powder
- ½ teaspoon of dry rosemary

DIRECTIONS

1. Rub the chicken with all of the listed spices and butter and let it sit for 30 minutes.
2. Add the forks to the spit and tighten the screws on the fork. Slide the chicken onto the spit and into the secured fork. Secure the chicken on the spit and insert the spit into the rotisserie connections.
3. Turn the function dial to 'Rotisserie' and set the timer to 50 minutes at 390°F.
4. Once done, remove and serve once slightly cooled by slicing.

ROTISSERIE BEEF CHUCK

Prep: 10 Minutes | Cooking Time: 50-60 Minutes | Makes: 2 Servings

INGREDIENTS

- 2 pounds of beef roast
- 1 teaspoon garlic powder
- 2 teaspoons onion salt
- 2 teaspoons parsley
- 4 teaspoons thyme
- 2 teaspoons basil
- 2 tablespoons of ghee
- Salt and black pepper, to taste

DIRECTIONS

1. First rub the meat with garlic powder, onion salt, parsley, thyme, basil, ghee, salt, and black pepper
2. Let it sit for 30 minutes.
3. Slide the beef chuck onto the spit and into the secured fork. Secure the chuck on the spit and insert the spit into the rotisserie connections.
4. Turn the function dial to 'Rotisserie' and set the timer to 50-60 minutes at 390°F.
5. Once done, remove and serve once slightly cooled by slicing

CAYENNE CHICKEN

Prep: 10 Minutes | Cooking Time: 65 Minutes | Makes: 2 Servings

INGREDIENTS

- 2 pounds of chicken, cut into 8 pieces
- Salt and black pepper, to taste
- 1 teaspoon of dried thyme
- 1 teaspoon of dried oregano
- 2 teaspoons of garlic powder
- 1 teaspoon of onion powder
- ½ teaspoon of smoked paprika

- 1/4 teaspoon of cayenne pepper
- Oil spray, for greasing

DIRECTIONS

1. Rub the chicken with the listed spices and lightly grease with oil spray.
2. Let it sit for 30 minutes in the refrigerator.
3. Now adjust the rotisserie shaft in the middle of the chicken and tie the legs of the chicken with twine.
4. Turn the function dial to 'Rotisserie' and set the timer to 65 minutes at 400°F.
5. Once done, let it cool and serve by slicing.

ZESTY CHICKEN

Prep: 10 Minutes | Cooking Time: 65 Minutes | Makes: 2 Servings

INGREDIENTS

- 2 pounds of whole chicken

RUB INGREDIENTS

- 4 tablespoons of ghee, organic
- 2 tablespoons of lemon juice
- 4 cloves of garlic, halved
- ½ teaspoon of smoked paprika
- 1 teaspoon garlic powder
- 1 teaspoon oregano powder
- Salt and black pepper, to taste

DIRECTIONS

1. Take a bowl and mix all of the rub ingredients with a fork.
2. Coat this rub all over the chicken.
3. Let it sit for 30 minutes in the refrigerator.
4. Slide the chicken onto the spit and into the secured fork. Secure the chicken on the spit and insert the spit into the rotisserie connections.
5. Turn the function dial to 'Rotisserie' and set the timer to 65 minutes at 400°F.
6. Once done, let it cool and serve by slicing.

TOP ROUND ROAST

Prep: 15 Minutes | Cooking Time: 65 Minutes | Makes: 3 Servings

INGREDIENTS

- 1.5-pounds of top round roast
- ¼ teaspoon crushed peppercorn
- Garlic herb mix
- Oil spray, for greasing

DIRECTIONS

1. Rub the top round roast with the peppercorn and garlic herb mix.
2. Grease with oil spray and insert into your air fryer rotisserie.
3. Put your roast on the rotisserie spit.
4. Turn the function dial to 'Rotisserie' and set it to 375°F for 65 minutes.
5. Remove the roast from the rotisserie shelf.
6. Allow to cool for 10 minutes before slicing and serving.

BEEF ROAST

Prep: 20 Minutes | Cooking Time: 65 Minutes | Makes: 2 Servings

INGREDIENTS

- 2 medium onions, sliced
- 3 cups white wine
- 3/4 cup olive oil
- 3 clove garlic, minced
- 1 tablespoon sea salt
- 1 tablespoon black pepper
- 1 teaspoon fresh rosemary, chopped
- 1 teaspoon celery seeds
- 1 teaspoon thyme leaves
- 1 teaspoon dried sage
- 2 tablespoons of unsalted butter
- 3 pounds beef roast

DIRECTIONS

1. Take a bowl and mix white wine, garlic, sea salt, rosemary, celery seeds, thyme, and sage.
2. Add this mixture to a large zip-lock plastic bag.
3. Add butter, beef, and onions.
4. Marinate overnight.
5. Once you are ready to start with the cooking, put the beef roast on the rotisserie spit.
6. Turn the function dial to 'Rotisserie' and set it to 400°F for 65 minutes.
7. Remove the roast from the rotisserie shelf.
8. Cool for 10 minutes before slicing and serving.

MARINATED BEEF ROAST

Prep: 15 Minutes | Cooking Time: 55 Minutes | Makes: 2 Servings

INGREDIENTS

- 1.5-pounds beef roast

MARINADE INGREDIENTS

- 1/3 cup white wine
- 1/2 tablespoon balsamic vinegar
- 2 tablespoons rosemary, fresh

STUFFING INGREDIENTS

- 1/3 cup onion, caramelized
- 1/3 cup spinach, frozen
- 1/2 tablespoon black pepper, freshly ground

DIRECTIONS

1. Mix all of the marinade ingredients in a bowl.
2. In a separate bowl mix all of the stuffing ingredients.
3. Now lay the beef on a clean flat surface and put the stuffing in the middle.
4. Roll the meat and secure it with some twine.
5. Coat the beef with the marinade and let it sit for 30 minutes in the refrigerator.
6. Put the beef roast on the rotisserie spit.

7. Turn the function dial to 'Rotisserie' and set it to 400°F for 55 minutes.
8. Remove the roast from the rotisserie shelf.
9. Allow to cool for 10 minutes before slicing and serving.

PERFECT RIB ROAST

Prep: 15 Minutes | Cooking Time: 65 Minutes | Makes: 2 Servings

INGREDIENTS

- 1/4 cup olive oil
- 4 tablespoons of Greek yogurt
- ¼ teaspoon of turmeric
- Salt and black pepper, to taste
- 1/6 teaspoon of thyme, powder
- ¼ teaspoon of garlic powder
- ¼ teaspoon of onion powder
- 12 prime ribs roast, trimmed

DIRECTIONS

1. Combine all of the listed ingredients in a large bowl and coat the prime rib well
2. Marinate the meat for 2 hours.
3. Thread the prime rib onto skewers and Slide the rib roast onto the spit and into the secured fork. Secure the rib roast on the spit and insert the spit into the rotisserie connections.
4. Turn the function dial to 'Rotisserie' and set the timer to 55-65 minutes at 400°F.
5. Once done, remove and serve once slightly cooled.

ALEPPO PRIME RIB

Prep: 10 Minutes | Cooking Time: 45-60 Minutes | Makes: 2 Servings

INGREDIENTS

- 2 pounds of prime rib roast, boneless
- Salt and black pepper, to taste
- 1 tablespoon garlic powder
- 2 tablespoons Aleppo pepper, powder
- 2 teaspoons of olive oil

DIRECTIONS

1. Mix all of the listed ingredients in a large bowl and coat the meat well.
2. Marinate the prime rib for 2 hours
3. Next, thread the prime rib and slide the rib onto the spit and into the secured fork. Secure the rib on the spit and insert the spit into the rotisserie connections.
4. Set the racks into the unit sockets.
5. Turn the function dial to 'Rotisserie' and set the timer to 55 minutes at 400°F.
6. Once done, remove and serve once slightly cooled.

BBQ PORK SPARE RIBS

Prep: 15 Minutes | Cooking Time: 55 Minutes | Makes: 4 Servings

INGREDIENTS

- 4 tablespoons of barbecue spice rub
- 1 tablespoon kosher salt and black pepper
- 3 tablespoons brown sugar
- 2 pounds pork spare-ribs, boneless
- 1 cup barbecue sauce
- Oil spray, for greasing

DIRECTIONS

1. Combine salt, black pepper, BBQ spice rub, and brown sugar in a bowl and mix well.
2. Lightly grease the rib with some oil spray and then rub the spice mixture all over the rib.
3. Slide the ribs onto the spit and into the secured fork. Secure the rib on the spit and insert the spit into the rotisserie connections.
4. Turn the function dial to 'Rotisserie' and set the timer to 55 minutes at 400°F.
5. Brush the rib with BBQ sauce after every 10 minutes of cooking.
6. Once done, remove and serve once slightly cooled.

DELICIOUS BEEF BACK RIB

Prep: 10 Minutes | Cooking Time: 45 Minutes | Makes: 2 Servings

INGREDIENTS

- Kosher salt, to taste
- 1 teaspoon onion powder
- ½ teaspoon of garlic powder
- Black pepper, to taste
- 2 pounds of beef back rib

DIRECTIONS

1. Peel the membrane out of the meat.
2. Mix all of the dry spices in a bowl and coat the beef back rib well.
7. Thread the beef onto the spit and into the secured fork. Secure the beef on the spit and insert the spit into the rotisserie connections.
3. Turn the function dial to 'Rotisserie' and set the timer to 45 minutes at 400°F.
4. Once done, remove and serve once slightly cooled.

BEEF BACK RIB

Prep: 10 Minutes | Cooking Time: 45-55 Minutes | Makes: 2 Servings

INGREDIENTS

- 2 tablespoons of lemon juice
- ¼ teaspoon of orange zest
- 1/4 cup fresh parsley, grated
- 4 large cloves of garlic, minced
- Salt, to taste
- Black pepper, to taste
- 12 beef back rib, trimmed

DIRECTIONS

1. Combine lemon juice, parsley, orange zest, garlic, salt, and pepper in a bowl and coat the beef rib.
2. Thread the rib onto the spit and into the secured fork. Secure the rib on

the spit and insert the spit into the rotisserie connections.
3. Turn the function dial to 'Rotisserie' and set the timer to 45-55 minutes at 400°F.
4. Once done, remove and serve once slightly cooled.

ROTISSERIE LAMB

Prep: 15 Minutes | Cooking Time: 45 Minutes | Makes: 4 Servings

INGREDIENTS

- 4 cloves of garlic
- 1 teaspoon of rosemary
- 1/3 cup extra virgin olive oil
- 1/4 cup fresh lemon juice
- ¼ teaspoon kosher salt
- ¼ teaspoon freshly ground black pepper
- ½ teaspoon lemon zest
- 2.5 pounds of a leg of lamb, boneless

FOR THE HERB BRUSH

- 4 sprigs of rosemary
- 7 tablespoons of melted butter
- 8 sprigs of thyme

DIRECTIONS

1. Take a bowl and whisk melted butter, rosemary, and thyme.
2. Rub the trimmed leg of lamb with lemon zest, black pepper, salt, lemon juice, rosemary, minced garlic, and olive oil.

3. Thread the lamb onto the spit and into the secured fork. Secure the lamb on the spit and insert the spit into the rotisserie connections.
4. Turn the function dial to 'Rotisserie' and set the timer to 65 minutes at 390°F.
5. Baste the lamb with the rosemary and thyme mixture every 15 minutes.
6. Once done, remove and serve once slightly cooled.

MEDITERRANEAN LAMB

Prep: 10 Minutes | Cooking Time: 55 Minutes | Makes: 2 Servings

INGREDIENTS

RUB INGREDIENTS

- 1 tablespoon garlic cloves, minced
- 1 tablespoon lemon juice, zest, and juice
- 2 tablespoon olive oil
- 1/4 teaspoons kosher salt and black pepper, to taste
- 2 tablespoons paprika
- 2 teaspoons coriander
- 1 teaspoon cumin
- 2 pounds of the leg of lamb

DIRECTIONS

1. Take a bowl and add all of the rub ingredients.

2. Coat the leg of lamb with the spice rub.
3. Let it sit for 30 minutes.
4. Thread the lamb onto the spit and into the secured fork. Secure the lamb on the spit and insert the spit into the rotisserie connections.
5. Turn the function dial to 'Rotisserie' and set the timer to 55-60 minutes at 390°F.
6. Once done, remove and serve once slightly cooled.

MARINATED LAMB LEG

Prep: 10 Minutes | Cooking Time: 55 Minutes | Makes: 2 Servings

INGREDIENTS

- 2 plum tomatoes, chopped
- 1 small yellow onion, chopped
- ½ cup dry red wine
- ½ cup Italian parsley leaves
- ½ cup loosely rosemary leaves
- 2 tablespoons Dijon mustard
- 2 large garlic cloves, crushed
- 1/4 teaspoon salt, to taste
- ¼ teaspoon black pepper, to taste

OTHER INGREDIENTS

- 2 pounds of boneless leg of lamb, trimmed

DIRECTIONS

1. Take a food processor and add all of the marinade ingredients to it.
2. Pulse until a paste is formed.
3. Marinade the lamb in the mixture for 30 minutes.
8. Thread the lamb onto the spit and into the secured fork. Secure the lamb on the spit and insert the spit into the rotisserie connections.
4. Turn the function dial to 'Rotisserie' and set the timer to 55-60 minutes at 390°F.
5. Once done, remove and serve once slightly cooled.

BEER GLAZED HAM

Prep: 10 Minutes | Cooking Time: 30 Minutes | Makes: 2 Servings

INGREDIENTS

- 3 pounds of ham
- 2 cups pineapple juice
- 1 cup 7-up
- 1 cup of dark beer
- ½ cup brown sugar
- 1 tablespoon salt
- 20 whole cloves

DIRECTIONS

1. Take a large saucepan and pour in pineapple juice, 7-up, dark beer, brown sugar, salt, and cloves.
2. Cook for 10 minutes on a medium heat to make the glaze.
3. Rub the ham with the glaze and let it marinate for 2 hours in the refrigerator.

9. Slide the ham onto the spit and into the secured fork. Secure the ham on the spit and insert the spit into the rotisserie connections.
4. Turn the function dial to 'Rotisserie' and set the timer to 30 minutes at 350°F.
5. After every 5 minutes brush the ham with the remaining glaze.
6. Once done, remove and serve once slightly cooled.

Pizza Recipes

Supreme Pizza
Page 103

Chorizo Pizza
Page 103

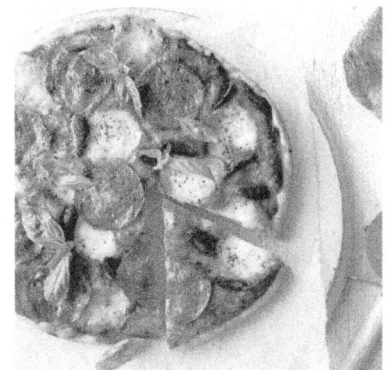
Salami Pizza
Page 105

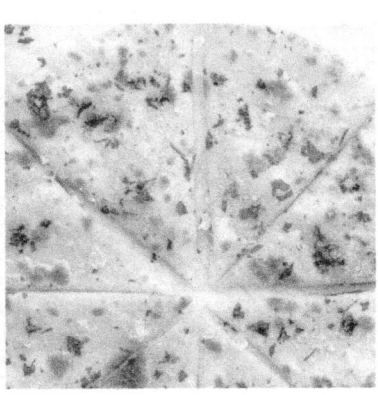
Garlic Pizza
Page 106

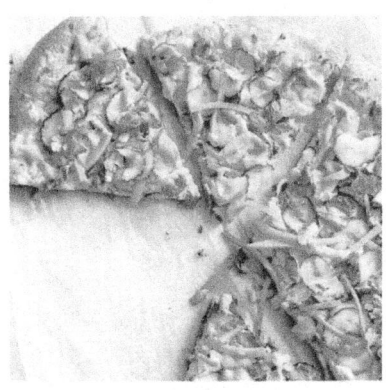
Veggies Pizza
Page 108

Three Cheese Pizza
Page 111

Meat Lover Pizza
Page 112

Seafood Pizza
Page 113

Grilled Chicken Pizza
Page 113

SUPREME PIZZA

Prep: 20 Minutes | Cooking Time: 20 Minutes | Makes: 2 Servings

INGREDIENTS

- 1 pizza dough, store-bought
- 2 tablespoon olive oil
- Topping ingredients
- 6 cremini mushrooms
- 6 slices of white onion
- 3 tablespoon pesto
- 2 cups shredded mozzarella
- 1 green pepper
- 1 cup spinach
- 12 slices of tomato

DIRECTIONS

1. Roll the pizza dough to the size of the grill plate on a flat surface.
2. Lightly oil both sides of the pizza dough and roll it onto grill plate.
3. Place the grill plate on the middle shelf of the air fryer.
4. Turn the function dial to 'Pizza' and cook at 400°F for 15 minutes.
5. Flip the dough and rotate the grill plate halfway through.
6. Afterwards, remove the grill plate from the air fryer and add mushrooms, pesto, white onion, green pepper, spinach, tomato, and cheese to the dough.
7. Place the grill plate back on its shelf.
8. Press the 'French Fries' button and cook at 400°F for 5 minutes.
9. Rotate the grill plate halfway through the cooking time.
10. Once done, serve.

CHORIZO PIZZA

Prep: 20 Minutes | Cooking Time: 15 Minutes | Makes: 2 Servings

INGREDIENTS

- 2 tablespoons of olive oil
- 13 ounces of thin-crust pizza dough

TOPPING INGREDIENTS

- 4 tablespoons basil pesto
- 1/2 cup pizza sauce
- 12 slice chorizo
- ½ yellow pepper, sliced
- 2 small red onion, sliced
- 12 slices of fresh mozzarella

DIRECTIONS

1. Roll the pizza dough to the size of the grill plate.
2. Lightly oil both sides of the pizza dough with olive oil and layer it onto the grill plate.
3. Place the grill plate on the top shelf of the air fryer.
4. Turn the function dial to 'Pizza' and cook at 400°F for 5 minutes.
5. Afterwards, remove the plate from the air fryer and add basil pesto, pizza sauce, chorizo, yellow pepper, red onion, and fresh mozzarella.
6. Place the plate back on the shelves.
7. Press the 'Pizza' button and cook at 400 °F for 5 minutes.

8. Rotate the plate halfway through the cooking time.
9. Once done, serve.

SIMPLE AIR FRYER PIZZA

Prep: 20 Minutes | Cooking Time: 20 Minutes | Makes: 2 Servings

INGREDIENTS

- 10 ounces of thin-crust pizza dough
- Oil spray, for greasing

TOPPING INGREDIENTS

- 1 small onion, chopped
- ½ red sweet pepper, sliced
- ½ yellow sweet pepper, sliced
- 3 chorizo links, cut bias
- 1/3 cup tomato sauce
- ½ cup jack cheese, shredded

DIRECTIONS

1. Roll out the dough on the oil-greased air fryer grill plate and grease the top with oil spray as well.
2. Place the plate on the top shelf and set it to pizza mode at 400 °F for 15 minutes.
3. Flip the dough and rotate the plate halfway through cooking.
4. Once done, take it out and add topping.
5. Place the grill plate back on its shelf.

6. Turn the function dial to 'Pizza' and cook at 400°F for 5 minutes.
7. Rotate the grill plate halfway through cooking.
8. Once done, serve.

WHITE PIZZA

Prep: 20 Minutes | Cooking Time: 16 Minutes | Makes: 2 Servings

INGREDIENTS

- 1 thin-crust pizza dough
- 1 tablespoon extra virgin olive oil

TOPPING INGREDIENTS

- ¼ cup ricotta cheese
- 7 slices of fresh mozzarella
- 2 cloves of garlic, thinly sliced
- 1 teaspoon red pepper flakes

DIRECTIONS

1. Rub both sides of the pizza dough with olive oil.
2. Roll the dough onto a grill plate.
3. Place grill plate on the middle shelf.
4. Press the 'Pizza' button and set it to 400°F for 10 minutes.
5. Flip halfway through the cooking time.
6. Afterwards, take out the pizza grill and top with all of the listed topping ingredients.
7. Put back into the air fryer and turn the function dial to 'Pizza' and cook at 400°F for 6 minutes.
8. Serve once the cheese has melted.

AIR FRYER PIZZA

Prep: 20 Minutes | Cooking Time: 16 Minutes | Makes: 2 Servings

INGREDIENTS

- 10 ounces fresh homemade pizza dough or store-bought

TOPPING INGREDIENTS

- 1/4 cup pizza sauce
- Pepperoni, as needed
- 1/2 cup mozzarella cheese, shredded
- Italian seasoning

DIRECTIONS

1. Grease the pizza dough with oil spray on both sides.
2. Roll the pizza dough onto the air fryer grill plate.
3. Place the plate on the middle shelf.
4. Press the 'Pizza' button and set it to 400°F for 5 minutes.
5. Flip halfway through.
6. Take out the dough and layer the pizza sauce along with a sprinkle of Italian seasoning, pepperoni, and mozzarella cheese.
7. Place back into the air fryer and turn the function dial to 'Pizza' and cook at 400°F for 10 minutes.
8. Serve once the cheese has melted.

SALAMI PIZZA

Prep: 20 Minutes | Cooking Time: 20 Minutes | Makes: 2 Servings

INGREDIENTS

- 1 store-bought pizza dough, thin-crust
- 2 tablespoons of vegetable oil

TOPPING INGREDIENT

- ½ cup of mozzarella, sliced thinly
- 50 grams salami, in strips
- 6 mushrooms, sliced
- 1 teaspoon dried oregano
- Freshly ground black pepper
- 4 tablespoons Parmesan cheese, grated
- A handful of fresh arugula.

DIRECTIONS

1. Grease the pizza dough with vegetable oil on both sides.
2. Roll the pizza dough onto the air fryer grill plate.
3. Place the grill plate on the middle shelf.
4. Press the 'Pizza' button and set the temperature to 400°F for 10 minutes.
5. Flip the dough and rotate the grill plate halfway through.
6. Take out the dough and add the toppings.
7. Put back into the air fryer and turn the function dial to 'Pizza' and cook at 400°F for 10 minutes.

8. Serve once the cheese has melted.

PEPPERONI PIZZA

Prep: 20 Minutes | Cooking Time: 15 Minutes | Makes: 2 Servings

INGREDIENTS

- 10 ounces store-bought pizza dough
- Oil spray for greasing

TOPPINGS

- 1/3 cup marinara
- ¼ cup mozzarella cheese, shredded
- ¼ cup cheddar cheese, shredded
- 10 slices of pepperoni
- 1 teaspoon chopped parsley

DIRECTIONS

1. Roll the pizza dough on a clean flat surface area.
2. Grease the pizza dough with oil spray on both sides.
3. Roll the pizza dough onto the air fryer grill plate.
4. Place plate on the top shelf.
5. Turn the function dial to 'Pizza' and set the temperature to 400°F for 8 minutes.
6. Flip the dough halfway through.
7. Take out the dough and pour marinara sauce all over.
8. Then add mozzarella cheese, cheddar cheese, and pepperoni slices.
9. Put back into the air fryer, and turn the function dial to 'Pizza' and cook at 400°F for 10 minutes.
10. Serve with a topping of chopped parsley.

GARLIC PIZZA

Prep: 20 Minutes | Cooking Time: 15 Minutes | Makes: 2 Servings

INGREDIENTS

- 12 ounces store-bought pizza dough
- 2 tablespoons of olive oil

INGREDIENTS FOR THE PIZZA SAUCE

- 250ml pizza sauce
- 2 tablespoons dried oregano
- 1 teaspoon garlic-infused oil
- Salt and pepper, to taste

INGREDIENTS FOR THE TOPPINGS

- 4 tablespoons mozzarella, sliced
- 1/3 cup fresh basil
- 2 tablespoons of olive oil

DIRECTIONS

1. Mix all of the pizza sauce ingredients in a bowl and set aside.
2. Roll the pizza dough on a clean flat surface.
3. Grease the pizza dough with olive oil on both sides.

4. Roll out the pizza dough onto the air baking pan.
5. Place pan on the middle shelf of the air fryer.
6. Turn the function dial to 'Pizza' and set the temperature to 400°F for 10 minutes.
7. Flip the dough and rotate the pan halfway through cooking.
8. Take out the dough and add the sauce.
9. Top with basil and mozzarella.
10. Place the airflow rack back on the middle shelf.
11. Turn the function dial to 'Pizza' and set the temperature to 400°F for 6 minutes.
12. Serve once the cheese has melted.
13. Drizzle with some additional olive oil over the top before serving.

MIX VEGETABLES PIZZA

Prep: 20 Minutes | Cooking Time: 25 Minutes | Makes: 2 Servings

INGREDIENTS

- 10 ounces store-bought thin-crust pizza dough
- Olive oil
- Salt, to taste

INGREDIENTS FOR PIZZA SAUCE

- 6 medium tomatoes, chopped
- 1 garlic clove, minced
- ½ cup olive oil
- 1 teaspoon of basil
- 1 teaspoon of oregano

TOPPING INGREDIENTS

- 1 onion, sliced
- 1 bell pepper, sliced
- 1 tomato, sliced
- 1 cup green olives, pitted
- ¼ cup kale, sautéed

DIRECTIONS

1. Roll out the pizza dough on a flat surface and lightly grease with olive oil.
2. Roll out the dough on the baking pan.
3. Place the pan on the middle shelf.
4. Turn the function dial to 'Pizza' and for 15 minutes at 400°F.
5. Meanwhile, take a saucepan and heat oil.
6. Add tomatoes, basil, oregano, and garlic cloves.
7. Let it cook until tomatoes are tender.
8. Add a few tablespoons of water if needed.
9. Once the dough is ready add the prepared sauce on top.
10. Then add all of the listed toppings one-by-one.
11. Place the pan back on the middle shelf.
12. Turn the function dial to 'Pizza' and set the temperature to 400°F for 6 minutes.
13. Serve once done.

CAULIFLOWER AND SPINACH PIZZA

Prep: 20 Minutes | Cooking Time: 15 Minutes | Makes: 2 Servings

INGREDIENTS

- 12 ounces of store-bought thin-crust pizza dough
- 2 tablespoons of olive oil

INGREDIENTS FOR TOPPINGS

- ½ cup marinara sauce
- 1 teaspoon of basil
- 1 teaspoon of oregano
- 1 onion, sliced
- 1 cup green olives, pitted
- ¼ cup spinach, sautéed
- 1 cup cauliflower, thawed
- 1 cup parmesan cheese

DIRECTIONS

1. Roll out the pizza dough on a flat surface and lightly grease with olive oil on both sides.
2. Roll out the dough onto the baking pan.
3. Place the pan on the top shelf.
4. Turn the function dial to 'Pizza' and set the timer for 8 minutes at 400°F using the pizza mode.
5. Remember to flip the dough halfway through/
6. Once the dough is ready, take it out.
7. Then add the entire listed toppings one-by-one.
8. Place the pan back on the middle shelf.
9. Turn the function dial to 'Pizza' and set the temperature to 400 °F for 6 minutes.
10. Serve once done.

VEGGIES PIZZA

Prep: 20 Minutes | Cooking Time: 15 Minutes | Makes: 2 Servings

INGREDIENTS

- 10 ounces of store-bought thin-crust pizza dough
- Salt, a few pinches
- 1 Japanese eggplant, cut into very thin round slices
- 1 cup yellow squash, thinly sliced
- 1 cup red onion, thinly sliced
- 1 yellow bell pepper, thinly sliced
- 3/4 cup pizza sauce
- 8 ounces mozzarella cheese, shredded

DIRECTIONS

1. First grease the dough of the pizza by flattening it on a clean surface on both sides with olive oil.
2. Roll out the dough on the air fryer baking pan.
3. Add to the middle shelf and press the pizza option.
4. Cook for 8 minutes at 400 degrees.
5. Remember to flip the dough halfway through.

6. Take out the dough and layer it with the pizza sauce.
7. Season with salt and add red onions, bell pepper, yellow squash, and eggplant slices.
8. Place the pan back onto the middle shelf.
9. Turn the function dial to 'Pizza' and cook for 6 minutes at 370°F.
10. Take out and sprinkle cheese on top.
11. Place back in the air fryer and choose pizza function and cook for 5 more minutes.
12. Once the cheese has melted, take it out and serve.

ARTICHOKE PIZZA

Prep: 20 Minutes | Cooking Time: 18 Minutes | Makes: 2 Servings

INGREDIENTS

- 12 ounces of store-bought pizza dough
- Oil spray, for greasing
- 1 cup marinara
- 2 cups baby spinach, thawed
- 2 cups mozzarella cheese
- ½ cup canned artichoke, cut into 1-inch pieces
- ½ cup bell pepper cut into 2 inches strips
- ½ cup red onion, cut into thin wedges
- ½ cup cherry tomatoes halved
- 1 teaspoon of red pepper flakes
- 1 cup Parmesan cheese

DIRECTIONS

1. Roll out the pizza dough on a flat surface and lightly grease with oil spray on both sides.
2. Then roll out the dough on the grill plate.
3. Place the plate on the middle shelf.
4. Turn the function dial to 'Pizza' and set the timer for 10 minutes at 400°F.
5. Remember to flip the dough halfway through,
6. Once the dough is ready, take it out and top it with marinara, baby spinach, artichokes, bell pepper, red onions, cherry tomatoes, mozzarella, and parmesan cheese.
7. Then season with red pepper flakes.
8. Put the plate back on the middle shelf.
9. Turn the function dial to 'Pizza' and set it to 400°F for 8 minutes.
10. Once the pizza is ready, serve, and enjoy.

EASY MIX VEGETABLE PIZZA

Prep: 20 Minutes | Cooking Time: 8 Minutes | Makes: 2 Servings

INGREDIENTS

- 10 ounces store-bought pizza dough

TOPPINGS

- 1 cup cream cheese
- ½ cup mayonnaise

- 1/2 teaspoon of dry ranch dressing
- 1 cup broccoli, raw
- 4 baby tomatoes
- ¼ cup of shredded carrots
- ½ cup of red bell peppers

DIRECTIONS

1. Roll the dough on an air fryer grill plate and grease with oil spray.
2. Flip the dough and grease the other side with oil spray.
3. Place the grill plate on the middle shelf and press the 'Power' button.
4. Turn the function dial to 'Pizza' and set it to 400°F for 8 minutes.
5. Flip the dough halfway through.
6. Meanwhile, mix mayonnaise, cream cheese, and ranch dressing in a bowl.
7. Once the dough is done, take it out and let it cool slightly.
8. Then add ranch layer along with remaining listed toppings.
9. Let it chill for a few minutes in the refrigerator before serving.

ULTIMATE VEGGIE PIZZA

Prep: 20 Minutes | Cooking Time: 22 Minutes | Makes: 2 Servings

INGREDIENTS

- 1 batch of store-bought pizza dough

TOPPING INGREDIENTS

- 1 cup pizza sauce or marinara sauce
- 2 cups baby spinach
- 2 cups shredded mozzarella cheese
- ½ cup fresh red or orange bell pepper cut into narrow 2" strips
- ½ cup red onion, cut into thin wedges
- ½ cups halved cherry tomatoes
- ½ cup pitted Kalamata olives, halved lengthwise
- ½ cup sliced almonds
- Few basil leaves
- Few pinches of Italian seasoning

DIRECTIONS

1. First, prepare the dough. For that roll the dough on a flat surface and grease with olive oil.
2. Roll out the dough on the grill plate and place it on the middle shelf.
3. Turn the function dial to 'Pizza' and set it to 360°F for 10 minutes.
4. Flip the dough halfway through.
5. Afterwards, take out the prepared dough and spread pizza sauce all over.
6. Then top with the listed toppings.
7. Place back in the air fryer.
8. Turn the function dial to 'Pizza' at 400°F for 12 minutes.
9. Once cheese has melted, serve the pizza.

THREE CHEESE PIZZA

Prep: 15 Minutes | Cooking Time: 18 Minutes | Makes: 2 Servings

INGREDIENTS

- 13 ounces of store-bought pizza dough
- 2 tablespoons of olive oil

TOPPING INGREDIENTS

- 1 cup marinara sauce
- ½ cups shredded mozzarella cheese
- ½ cup shredded parmesan
- ½ cup ricotta cheese
- Few basil leaves

DIRECTIONS

1. Roll the dough on a flat surface and grease with olive oil on both sides.
2. Roll out the dough on the baking pan and place it on the middle shelf.
3. Turn the function dial to 'Pizza' and set it to 360°F for 10 minutes.
4. Flip the dough halfway through.
5. Afterward, take out the prepared dough and spread the marinara sauce all over.
6. Then spread the cheeses on top.
7. Add a few basil leaves.
8. Place the pizza back into the air fryer.
9. Turn the function dial to 'Pizza' to 400°F for 8 minutes.
10. Once the cheese has melted, serve the pizza.

SAUSAGE PIZZA

Prep: 15 Minutes | Cooking Time: 20 Minutes | Makes: 2 Servings

INGREDIENTS

- 12 ounces pizza dough, store-bought crust
- ½ cup marinara sauce
- 12 ounces spicy sausage, cooked and crumbled
- ¼ cup thinly sliced onion
- 2 cups shredded mozzarella cheese
- 1 tablespoon chilli oil
- Black pepper, to taste

DIRECTIONS

1. Roll the dough on a flat surface and grease with olive oil on both sides.
2. Roll out the dough on the baking pan and place it on the middle shelf.
3. Turn the function dial to 'Pizza' and set it to 360°F for 10 minutes.
4. Flip the dough halfway through.
5. Afterward, take out the prepared dough and spread the marinara sauce all over.
6. Top with the sausage, onion, and mozzarella cheese.
7. Drizzle chilli oil and sprinkle with pepper.
8. Place the plate back inside the air fryer.
9. Turn the function dial to 'Pizza' and use the 'Pizza' mode at 400°F for 8 minutes.
10. Once the cheese has melted, serve the pizza.

ITALIAN SAUSAGE PIZZA

Prep: 20 Minutes | Cooking Time: 15 Minutes | Makes: 2 Servings

INGREDIENTS

- 10 ounces of thin-crust pizza dough

TOPPING INGREDIENTS

- 4 hot Italian sausages, cooked and cubed
- 1/2 cup sliced onion
- 1/2 cup mushrooms, chopped
- 1/2 cup pizza sauce
- 2 cups parmesan cheese
- 2 tablespoons of chilli oil
- Black pepper, to taste

DIRECTIONS

1. Roll the dough on a flat surface and grease with olive oil on both sides.
2. Roll out the dough on the grill plate and layer with pizza sauce, Italian sausage, raw onion, mushrooms, and parmesan cheeses.
3. Drizzle chilli oil and a sprinkle of pepper.
4. Place the plate back inside the air fryer.
5. Turn the function dial to 'Pizza' and use the 'Pizza' mode and 'French Fries' mode at 400°F for 15 minutes.
6. Once the cheese has melted, serve the pizza.

MEAT LOVER PIZZA

Prep: 20 Minutes | Cooking Time: 18 Minutes | Makes: 2 Servings

INGREDIENTS

- 10 ounces of pizza dough, store-bought
- 2 tablespoons of olive oil

TOPPINGS

- 1/3 cup pizza sauce
- 1 cup mozzarella cheese, shredded
- ½ cup sausage, cooked and crumbled
- 10 pepperoni slices
- 6 slices of bacon, cooked and sliced

4 tablespoons Parmesan cheese, shredded

DIRECTIONS

1. Roll the dough on a flat surface and grease with olive oil on both sides.
2. Roll out the dough on the baking pan and place it on the middle shelf.
3. Turn the function dial to 'Pizza' and set it to 360°F for 10 minutes.
4. Flip the dough halfway through.
5. Afterward, take out the prepared dough and spread pizza sauce all over it.
6. Then top with the toppings.
7. Place the baking pan back inside the air fryer.

8. Turn the function dial to 'Pizza' and use the 'Pizza' mode at 400°F for 8 minutes.
9. Once the cheese has melted, serve the pizza.

SEAFOOD PIZZA

Prep: 15 Minutes | Cooking Time: 19 Minutes | Makes: 2 Servings

INGREDIENTS

- 8 ounces pizza crust, store-bought
- Oil spray

TOPPING INGREDIENTS

- 6 uncooked shrimp, shells removed
- 6 tablespoons of pizza sauce
- 4 ounces shredded mozzarella cheese
- ½ cup shredded provolone cheese
- 1/3 cup of scallops
- ½ cup chopped fresh basil leaves
- Few garlic cloves, chopped

DIRECTIONS

1. Roll the dough on a flat surface and grease it with olive oil on both sides.
2. Roll out the dough on the baking pan and then place it on the middle shelf.
3. Turn the function dial to 'Pizza' and set it to 360°F for 10 minutes.
4. Flip the dough halfway through.
5. Afterward, take out the prepared dough and spread pizza sauce all over.
6. Then top with scallops, shrimp, mozzarella cheese, provolone cheese, garlic, and basil.
7. Place the pan back inside the air fryer.
8. Turn the function dial to 'Pizza' and use the 'Pizza' mode at 400°F for 9 minutes.
9. Once the cheese has melted, serve the pizza.

GRILLED CHICKEN PIZZA

Prep: 20 Minutes | Cooking Time: 15 Minutes | Makes: 2 Servings

INGREDIENTS

- 1 cup of grilled chicken breasts, cut into 1-inch pieces
- 1 tablespoon olive oil
- 10 inches pizza crust
- 1/3 cup prepared pesto
- 1 large tomato, chopped
- 1 cup shredded mozzarella cheese

DIRECTIONS

1. Roll the dough on a flat surface and grease with olive oil on both sides.
2. Roll out the dough on the baking pan and then place it on the middle shelf.
3. Turn the function dial to 'Pizza' and set it to 360°F for 10 minutes.

4. Flip the dough halfway through.
5. Afterward, take out the prepared dough and spread pesto all over it.
6. Then top with grilled chicken, tomatoes, and mozzarella cheese.
7. Place baking pan back inside the air fryer.
8. Turn the function dial to 'Pizza' at 400°F for 9 minutes.
9. Once cheese has melted, serve the pizza.

Dessert Recipes

Super Moist Cupcake
Page 119

Vanilla Cupcake
Page 120

Pignoli Cookies
Page 121

Raisin and Oatmeal Cookies
Page 123

Vanilla Bean Meringues
Page 124

Empanada Wraps
Page 126

Ginger Cranberry Scones
Page 127

Mint and Chocolate Pudding
Page 128

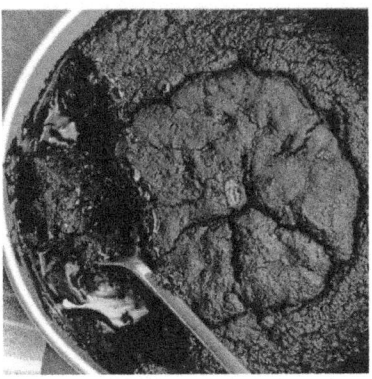

Chocolate Pudding Cake
Page 128

MINI CHOCOLATE PEANUT BUTTER CUPCAKES

Prep: 10 Minutes | Cooking Time: 15 Minutes | Makes: 2 Servings

INGREDIENTS

- 1 large egg
- ½ cup whole milk
- 1 cup vegetable oil
- ¼ teaspoon vanilla extract
- ½ cup flour
- 1 cup sugar
- ¼ cup cocoa
- 1 teaspoon baking powder
- 1/4 teaspoon salt
- ¼ cup water

PEANUT BUTTER FROSTING INGREDIENTS

- 1 sticks unsalted butter
- 2 cups confectioners' sugar
- 1 tablespoon whole milk
- Few chocolate pearls

DIRECTIONS

1. Whisk eggs in a bowl and add milk, oil, and vanilla extract.
2. Then combine flour with sugar, cocoa, baking powder, salt and mix well in a separate bowl.
3. Add water to the flour mixture and slowly add in the whisked egg mixture.
4. Pour this mixture into an aluminum cupcake tray lined with cupcake liners.
5. Place the cupcake tray on the baking tray.
6. Adjust the tray on the top shelf.
7. Turn the function dial to 'Bake' for 15 minutes at 350°F.
8. Rotate the baking tray halfway through.
9. Meanwhile, mix all of the Peanut Butter Frosting ingredients to make the frosting.
10. Then layer it on top of the cupcakes.
11. Serve and enjoy.

SUPER MOIST CUPCAKE

Prep: 10 Minutes | Cooking Time: 15 Minutes | Makes: 2 Servings

INGREDIENTS

- 150 grams all-purpose flour
- 80 grams cocoa powder
- ½ teaspoon baking powder
- 1/4 teaspoon baking soda
- 1/4 teaspoon salt
- 2 large eggs, organic
- 1/2 cup granulated sugar
- 1/2 cup light brown sugar
- ½ cups coconut oil
- 1 teaspoon pure vanilla extract
- 1/2 cup buttermilk

DIRECTIONS

1. Whisk eggs in a bowl and add sugar and brown sugar.
2. Then whisk in the buttermilk and vanilla extract.
3. In a separate bowl mix all of the remaining dry ingredients.
4. Now pour the egg mixture into the dry ingredients.
5. A smooth batter will be formed.
6. Add the oil.
7. Mix well into the batter.
8. Pour this mixture into an aluminum cupcake tray lined with cupcake liners.
9. Place the cupcake tray on the grill plate
10. Adjust the plate on the top shelf.
11. Turn the function dial to 'Bake' for 15 minutes at 350°F.
12. Rotate the grill plate halfway through.
13. Meanwhile, mix all of the reaming ingredients to make the frosting
14. Then add it to the top of cupcakes.
15. Serve and enjoy.

VANILLA CUPCAKE

Prep: 12 Minutes | Cooking Time: 15 Minutes | Makes: 2 Servings

INGREDIENTS

- 250 grams of sugar
- 220 grams of butter
- 4 eggs
- 1/2 cup almond milk
- 210 grams all-purpose flour
- 1/4 cup rainbow sprinkles
- 1/4 tablespoon vanilla extract

DIRECTIONS

1. Whisk butter, vanilla, and sugar.
2. Then crack in the egg and whisk all of the ingredients with a hand mixer.
3. Fold in the milk and flour and mix with a spatula.
4. Then add in the sprinkles.
5. Spoon this batter into a silicone cupcake holder and put it on to baking tray.
6. Place the baking tray inside the unit and turn dial to 'Bake' at 350°F for 15 minutes.
7. Serve and enjoy.

FUDGE BROWNIES

Prep: 20 Minutes | Cooking Time: 18 Minutes | Makes: 4 Servings

INGREDIENTS

- 1/2 cup all-purpose flour
- 1/4 cup unsweetened cocoa powder
- 3/4 teaspoon kosher salt
- 2 large eggs, whisked
- 1 tablespoon almond milk
- 1/2 cup brown sugar
- 1/2 cup packed white sugar
- 1/2 tablespoon vanilla extract
- 8 ounces of semisweet chocolate chips, melted
- 2/4 cup unsalted butter, melted

DIRECTIONS

1. Take a bowl and whisk eggs, milk, all of the sugar, salt, and vanilla.

2. Melt chocolate with butter in the microwave.
3. Now add dry ingredients to a separate bowl.
4. Now pour the egg mixture into the bowl.
5. Now add the chocolate mixture to the bowl.
6. Mix and incorporate all of the ingredients.
7. Take a baking pan and grease it with oil spray.
8. Pour the batter into the baking pan.
9. Place it on the bottom shelf.
10. Close the unit.
11. Turn the dial to 'Bake' for 18 minutes at 350°F.
12. Remember to rotate halfway through cooking.
13. Once done, serve, and enjoy.

PIGNOLI COOKIES

Prep: 10 Minutes | Cooking Time: 15 Minutes | Makes: 4 Servings

INGREDIENTS

- 10 ounces almond butter
- ½ cup sugar
- 4 large egg whites
- 1 cup confectioner's sugar
- 2 cups pine nuts

DIRECTIONS

1. Use a hand beater and make an almond paste with sugar.
2. Now, beat two egg whites and add to the almond paste mixture.
3. Then add the confectioners' sugar.
4. Mix very well and make into dough.
5. Now whisk the remaining egg whites in a separate bowl and add to the batter.
6. Shape the dough into one-inch balls.
7. Coat each ball with pine nuts.
8. Place the balls on a baking tray lined with parchment paper.
9. Place the tray on the bottom shelf.
10. Turn the dial to 'Bake' at 390°F for 15 minutes.
11. Remember to rotate halfway through.
12. Serve and enjoy.

LEMONY SWEET TWISTS

Prep: 15 Minutes | Cooking Time: 10 Minutes | Makes: 2 Servings

INGREDIENTS

- 1 package of store-bought puff pastry
- ½ teaspoon lemon zest
- 1/2 tablespoon of lemon juice
- 4 teaspoons brown sugar
- Salt, pinch
- 4 tablespoons Parmesan cheese, grated

DIRECTIONS

1. Put the puff pastry on a clean, flat surface.
2. Take a bowl and mix sugar, salt, lemon zest, lemon juice, and cheese.

3. Now spread this mixture on both ends of the dough.
4. Press it into both sides of the dough.
5. Cut the pastry into 1" x 6" strips.
6. Twist it into strips.
7. Transfer it to the air fryer baking pan.
8. Turn on the dial function to 'Bake' at 400°F for 12 minutes.
9. Once cooked, serve, and enjoy.

JAM FILLED BUTTERMILK SCONES

Prep: 10 Minutes | Cooking Time: 18 Minutes | Makes: 4 Servings

INGREDIENTS

2 cups of flour
Salt, to taste
1/3 cup sugar
2 teaspoons baking powder
12 tablespoon butter
3 large eggs
1/3 cup buttermilk
1 teaspoon vanilla extract
½ cup strawberry jam

DIRECTIONS

1. Mix salt, sugar, salt, baking powder, and flour in a large bowl and set aside.
2. Whisk eggs in a separate large bowl and add buttermilk, vanilla extract.
3. Grate the butter and toss the butter into the flour mixture.
4. Mix well.
5. Now stir in the egg mixture.
6. Roll into a dough and make into two discs from the dough.
7. Wraps the discs in a plastic wrapper and place in the refrigerator for 1 hour.
8. Layer the discs on a flat surface.
9. Top with strawberry jam.
10. Take the second disc and place it on top of the first disc and seal the edges.
11. Cut the dough into eight wedges.
12. Seal the edges well.
13. Place the wedges on the baking tray lined with parchment paper.
14. Brush the wedges generously with buttermilk.
15. Put the tray on the bottom shelf.
16. Turn the function dial to 'Bake' at 375°F for 15-18 minutes.
17. Remember to flip halfway through.
18. Once done, serve.
19. Enjoy.

CINNAMON SWEET TWISTS

Prep: 10 Minutes | Cooking Time: 12 Minutes | Makes: 4 Servings

INGREDIENTS

1 store-bought puff pastry
½ teaspoon cinnamon
1 teaspoon sugar
1 teaspoon black sesame seeds
Salt, pinch
2 tablespoons Parmesan cheese, freshly grated

DIRECTIONS

1. Place the dough on a flat surface.
2. In a bowl mix sugar, salt, sesame seeds, cinnamon, and cheese.
3. Now press this mixture on both sides of the dough.
4. Cut the pastry into 8 strips.
5. Twist the strips.
6. Place the strips on the baking tray.
7. Put the tray on the middle shelf.
8. Turn the dial to 'Air Fry' at 400°F for 12 minutes.
9. Remember to flip it halfway through.
10. Once cooked, serve.

RAISIN AND OATMEAL COOKIES

Prep: 20 Minutes | Cooking Time: 18 Minutes | Makes: 4 Servings

INGREDIENTS

- 1 cup unsalted butter
- 1 cup brown sugar, packed
- 1/3 cup tablespoons granulated sugar
- 3 large eggs
- ½ tablespoon vanilla extract
- 1 1/2 cups all-purpose flour
- Salt, pinch
- 1 teaspoon baking soda
- ½ teaspoon ground cinnamon
- ¼ teaspoon freshly grated nutmeg
- 1 1/4 cups raisins
- 1/3 cup chopped walnuts (optional)
- 3 cups rolled oats

DIRECTIONS

1. Mix butter, sugar, brown sugar, and eggs.
2. Use a hand beater to beat the ingredients.
3. Add in the vanilla extract.
4. Now mix all of the dry ingredients in a separate bowl.
5. Shift the egg mixture into the flour. Add the remaining ingredients.
6. Mix well for fine incorporation.
7. Stir well and then scoop the dough on the oil-greased baking sheet in the shape of cookie dough.
8. Leave two inches of space in between.
9. Place the sheet on the lower shelf.
10. Close the unit.
11. Turn the dial to 'Air Fry' for 18 minutes at 350°F.
12. Serve.

CREAM PUFFS

Prep: 15 Minutes | Cooking Time: 40 Minutes | Makes: 2 Servings

INGREDIENTS

½ cup whole milk
2 tablespoons sugar
Salt, pinch
2 tablespoon butter
½ cup flour
3 organic eggs
½ cup vanilla pudding, cooked

DIRECTIONS

1. Whisk milk along with butter, a pinch of salt, and sugar in a saucepan.
2. Bring the mixture to a boil.
3. Now let it cool and add in the flour.
4. Now use a bowl mixture and add it to the mixing bowl and attach a stand mixture to it.
5. Mix it on a low setting and add one egg at a time to form dough.
6. Pipe this dough into rounds using a large rounded tip.
7. Layer it onto the baking tray lined with two pieces of parchment paper.
8. Place the tray on the lower unit.
9. Turn the dial to 'Bake' and set it to 350°F for 35 minutes.
10. Once done, take it out and let it cool.
11. Place a hole in the bottom of each puff.
12. Fill the puff with vanilla pudding.
13. Serve and enjoy.

CHOCOLATE FILLED CREAM PUFFS

Prep: 15 Minutes | Cooking Time: 20 Minutes | Makes: 4 Servings

INGREDIENTS

- ½ cup almond milk
- 2 tablespoons brown sugar
- 2 tablespoons almond butter
- ½ cup all-purpose flour
- 2 organic eggs
- 1 cup chocolate sauce

DIRECTIONS

1. Take a saucepan and add almond milk, butter, and sugar to it.
2. Bring it to a boil.
3. Then let it cool.
4. Add flour to the milk mixture and mix well.
5. Let it cool.
6. Now start adding eggs one at a time to the mixture.
7. Once the dough is formed, place the dough onto a flat surface.
8. Pipe this dough into rounds using a large rounded tip.
9. Layer it onto the baking tray lined with two parchment papers.
10. Place the baking tray on the lower shelf of the unit.
11. Turn the function dial to 'Bake' and set it to 350°F for 35 minutes.
12. Rotate the rack after 20 minutes.
13. Place a hole in the bottom of each puff.
14. Fill the puff with chocolate sauce.
15. Serve and enjoy.

VANILLA BEAN MERINGUES

Prep: 15 Minutes | Cooking Time: 3 Hours 30 Minutes | Makes: 2 Servings

INGREDIENTS

- 1/3 cup sugar, granulated
- Salt, to taste
- 5 extra-large egg whites
- 1 vanilla bean, seeds extracted

DIRECTIONS

1. Take a bowl and add the egg whites.
2. Whisk using a hand mixer at a medium speed.
3. Once frothy add in the sugar, salt, and vanilla seeds and increase the speed.
4. Once a stiff peak forms on the top, transfer it to a piping bag with a star tip.
5. Line a parchment paper on the baking tray and start piping the mixture onto the rack, while keeping a distance between each meringue.
6. Put the tray in the middle of the air fryer.
7. Turn the dial to 'Bake' at 375°F for 20 minutes.
8. Once it's done, take it out and let it cool before serving.

LEMON MERINGUES

Prep: 10 Minutes | Cooking Time: 3 Hours 30 Minutes | Makes: 4 Servings

INGREDIENTS

- 4 eggs, whites only
- 1/2 teaspoon cream of tartar
- Pinch of salt
- ½ cup granulated sugar
- ½ teaspoon lemon extract

DIRECTIONS

1. Mix salt, fine sugar, and egg whites in a bowl.
2. Whisk using a hand mixer at a medium speed.
3. Once frothy add in the cream of tartar and lemon extract.
4. Mix again until a stiff peak forms on top.
5. Transfer to a piping bag with a star tip.
6. Line a parchment paper on the baking tray and start piping the mixture onto the rack, keeping a distance between each meringue.
7. Put the tray on the middle of the air fryer.
8. Turn the dial to 'Bake' at 375°F for 20 minutes.
9. Once it's done, take it out and let it cool before serving.

COCONUT MERINGUES

Prep: 10 Minutes | Cooking Time: 3 Hours 30 Minutes | Makes: 2 Servings

INGREDIENTS

¼ teaspoon cream of tartar
Pinch of salt
3 large egg whites
½ cup sugar, granulated
¼ teaspoon vanilla extract
⅛ Teaspoon coconut extract

DIRECTIONS

1. Mix cream of tartar, salt, vanilla extract, and egg whites in a large bowl.
2. Beat with a hand beater.

3. Once stiff peaks form on the top add in the sugar.
4. Beat it until the sugar dissolves.
5. Next, add the coconut extract and mix until combined.
6. Drop a tablespoon of this mixture onto the baking tray lined with parchment paper.
7. Put the tray in the middle of the air fryer.
8. Turn the dial to 'Air Fry' and set the temperature to 170°F for 3 hours for 30 minutes.
9. Once it's done, take it out and let it cool before serving.

SWEET POTATO MUG CAKE FOR TWO

Prep: 10 Minutes | Cooking Time: 5 Minutes | Makes: 2 Servings

INGREDIENTS

- 1/2 cup sweet potato, cooked and mashed
- 4 tablespoons almond butter
- 2 eggs
- 1 teaspoon cinnamon
- 2 tablespoons Stevia
- 1/2 cup of chocolate chips
- 1/2 cup Greek yogurt, for topping

DIRECTIONS

1. Mash the potatoes in a bowl and add almond butter, eggs, Stevia, cinnamon, and chocolate chips.
2. Mix well and pour into oil-greased ramekins.
3. Place ramekins on the baking tray and place it on the middle shelf.
4. Turn the dial to 'Air Fry' and set the timer to cook for 5 minutes at 325°F.
5. Top with yogurt and serve.

EMPANADA WRAPS

Prep: 15 Minutes | Cooking Time: 10 Minutes | Makes: 5 Servings

INGREDIENTS

- 10 empanada wrappers, thawed
- 2 apples
- 4 tablespoons raw honey
- 1 teaspoon vanilla extract
- ½ teaspoon cinnamon
- 1/8 teaspoon nutmeg
- 3 teaspoons cornstarch
- 2 teaspoons water
- 1 egg, beaten, for coating
- Oil spray, for greasing

DIRECTIONS

1. Take a saucepan and add apples, honey, vanilla extract, cinnamon, nutmeg, and cook for 2 minutes.
2. Then mix cornstarch in water and add it to the sauce.
3. Let it cook for 1 minute.
4. Let it cool completely.
5. Now wet the empanada wrapper with egg wash using a brush on the edges.
6. Put some apple mixture in each empanada.

7. Close the empanadas.
8. Use a fork to seal the edges by pressing the fork down along the edges.
9. Grease the baking pan with oil spray.
10. Put the wrappers on the baking pan.
11. Place the pan on the top shelf.
12. Turn the dial to 'Air Fry' and set the temperature to 400°F for 10 minutes
13. Once done, serve.

MINI STRAWBERRY AND CREAM PIES

Prep: 10 Minutes | Cooking Time: 12 Minutes | Makes: 4 Servings

INGREDIENTS

- 1 box store-bought Trader Joe's pie dough
- 1 cup strawberries, cubed
- 3 tablespoons of heavy cream
- 2 tablespoons of almonds
- 1 egg white, for brushing

DIRECTIONS

1. Flatten the pie dough on a flat clean work area.
2. Cut into 4-inch circles using a round cutter.
3. Brush the dough with egg white around the edges.
4. Put almonds, strawberries, and cream in the center of the dough.
5. Top it with one more circular piece of dough.

6. Press the edges and seal with a fork.
7. Place on a baking pan and add to the bottom rack of the air fryer.
8. Close the unit.
9. Turn the dial to 'Air Fry' and set it to 400°F for 10 -12 minutes.
10. Once ready, take it out and serve.

GINGER CRANBERRY SCONES

Prep: 15 Minutes | Cooking Time: 15 Minutes | Makes: 4 Servings

INGREDIENTS

- 2 cups all-purpose flour
- 1/4 cup dark brown sugar
- 1.5 teaspoon baking powder
- 1.5 teaspoon cinnamon
- 1/2 teaspoon freshly ground nutmeg
- 1/4 teaspoon cloves
- 1/4 teaspoon salt
- Pinch of ginger powder
- 1/3 cup dried cranberries
- 12 tablespoons unsalted butter, frozen, grated on a box grater
- 1/3 cup heavy cream, plus more for glazing
- 1 teaspoon canola oil
- 2 large eggs
- 1 teaspoon vanilla extract
- ¼ cup sour cream
- Demerara sugar, for sprinkling

DIRECTIONS

1. Mix flour, sugar, baking soda, baking powder, nutmeg, cinnamon, salt, cloves, ginger, and cranberries in a bowl and mix well.
2. Then add the butter.
3. In a separate bowl mix heavy cream, egg, vanilla, cream.
4. Add wet ingredients to the dry ingredients.
5. Make the dough into a circle ¾" in thickness.
6. Cut the dough into 8 wedges.
7. Brush the top of the wedge with oil and Demerara sugar.
8. Place onto the baking pan.
9. Place the racks on the top shelf.
10. Turn on the dial to 'Bake' for 15 minutes at 365°F.
11. Rotate the baking pan halfway through.
12. Serve and enjoy.

MINT AND CHOCOLATE PUDDING

Prep: 10 Minutes | Cooking Time: 12 Minutes | Makes: 2 Servings

INGREDIENTS

- 2 tablespoons chocolate pudding
- 10 ounces Greek yogurt
- 2 mint chocolate cookies
- ¼ teaspoon of mint extract

DIRECTIONS

1. Grease the ramekins with oil spray.
2. Mix the cookies with mint extract and microwave for 2 minutes.
3. Then put the mixture into the ramekins.
4. Mix yogurt with pudding in a bowl.
5. Put it on top of the ramekin mixture.
6. Place the ramekins onto the baking pan.
7. Place the baking pans on the middle shelf.
8. Turn the dial to 'Bake' and set the temperature to 300°F for 12 minutes.
9. Once it's done, serve.

CHOCOLATE PUDDING CAKE

Prep: 10 Minutes | Cooking Time: 12 Minutes | Makes: 2 Servings

INGREDIENTS

- ½ tablespoon butter
- ½ cup milk chocolate
- 2 eggs
- ¼ teaspoon of baking powder
- 2 tablespoons of sugar, to taste
- 1 cup of flour, all-purpose
- Oil spray, for greasing

DIRECTIONS

1. Take a bowl and whisk the eggs.
2. Then add butter, milk chocolate, and sugar.
3. Then add in all-purpose flour and baking soda.
4. Now grease the ramekins with oil spray.

5. Pour the pudding into the ramekins.
6. Cover the ramekins with cling film.
7. Put onto the baking pan.
8. Turn the dial to 'Bake' and set the temperature to 350°F for 12 minutes.
9. Serve and enjoy.

VANILLA CAKE

Prep: 15 Minutes | Cooking Time: 30 Minutes | Makes: 2 Servings

INGREDIENTS

- 90 grams all-purpose flour
- Pinch of salt
- 1/2 teaspoon of baking powder
- 2 eggs
- 1 teaspoon of vanilla extract
- 10 tablespoons of white sugar

DIRECTIONS

1. Put the all-purpose flour, salt, and baking powder in a bowl.
2. Take a separate bowl and whisk eggs along with vanilla extract, sugar and mix well.
3. Now mix wet ingredients with the dry ones.
4. Pour it into a round pan.
5. Put the pan on a baking pan.
6. Place it on a baking pan and put it inside the unit.
7. Turn the function dial to 'Air Crisp' mode at 25 -30 minutes at 350°F.
8. Once done, serve and enjoy.

GRILLED PINEAPPLE

Prep: 10 Minutes | Cooking Time: 10 Minutes | Makes: 2 Servings

INGREDIENTS

- 2 cups pineapple, sliced

DIRECTIONS

1. Insert the grill plate in the PowerXL Air Fryer Grill and preheat for 10 minutes at 400°F.
2. Add the pineapple to the grill plate.
3. Grill it for 10 minutes at 350°F.
4. Flip halfway through.
5. Once it's done serve.

GRILLED BANANAS

Prep: 10 Minutes | Cooking Time: 8 minutes | Makes: 2 Servings

INGREDIENTS

- 4 bananas, sliced, Peel, cut in half lengthwise
- ½ tablespoon cinnamon
- Salt, pinch

DIRECTIONS

1. Turn the dial function to 400°F for 10 minutes on the 'Grill' mode.
2. Sprinkle cinnamon and salt over the bananas.

3. Put the banana slices on the grill grate.
4. Turn the dial to the 'Grill' function at 400°F for 8 minutes.
5. Flip it halfway through.
6. Once done, serve.

GRILLED APPLE

Prep: 10 Minutes | Cooking Time: 12 Minutes | Makes: 2 Servings

INGREDIENTS

- 2 apples, sliced, peeled, cut in half lengthwise
- ½ tablespoon cinnamon
- Salt, pinch

DIRECTIONS

1. Turn the dial function to 400°F for 10 minutes on the 'Grill' mode.
2. Sprinkle cinnamon and salt over sliced apples.
3. Put the banana slices on the grill grate.
4. Turn the dial to the 'Grill' function at 400°F for 12 minutes.
5. Flip it halfway through.
6. Once done, serve.

CHOCLATE CHIP CUPCAKE

Prep: 12 Minutes | Cooking Time: 15 Minutes | Makes: 2 Servings

INGREDIENTS

- 250 grams of brown sugar
- 220 grams of butter
- 4 eggs
- 1/2 cup coconut milk
- 210 grams all-purpose flour
- ½ cup chocolate chip

DIRECTIONS

1. Whisk egg, butter, vanilla, and sugar with a hand mixer.
2. Pour in the milk and flour and mix with a spatula.
3. Then add in the chocolate chips.
4. Spoon this batter into a silicone cupcake holder
5. Put it on the baking tray.
6. Put it inside the unit and turn the dial to 'Bake' at 350°F for 15 minutes.
7. Serve and enjoy.

What Else?

Grab "Italian Copycat recipes" for free!

Do you love to eat at Carrabba's, Maggiano's Little Italy, or Olive Garden? What if I told you that you can cook all of those great and delicious Italian dishes of your favorite restaurants at your home, without failing, without spending a lot of money, and make them even healthier?

I think we all love delicious food.

Eating, talking, and spending time with our family and friends in front of the lunch or dinner table. And, of course, if food is good, it makes that time together even more pleasant, more vibrant, and creates a well-rounded combination altogether.

Meanwhile, if food is not good, it can almost destroy all of the pleasure and happiness of these gatherings – that's why most people choose a restaurant to get proven and tasty food and refuse to take that risk of home-cooking, even though eating out is more expensive and time-consuming.

I have put together proven recipes of the world's most famous Italian restaurant chains so that you can use them for cooking these amazing dishes yourself.

Discover over 100 delicious Italian recipes from world-famous Italian restaurants:

- Buca Di Beppo™
- Olive Garden™
- Bertucci's™

- California Pizza Kitchen™
- Carrabba's™
- The Old Spaghetti Factory™
- Romano's Macaroni Grill™
- Maggiano's Little Italy™

You don't have to be a world-class chef to cook these great dishes, not even close. This book will tell you everything in a simple way and lead you through every single step!

- **Complete instructions** with a detailed list of ingredients
- **Cooking and preparation times** with the number of servings
- **Extra cooking guidelines** to make sure you succeed every time
- **Dessert and side dish recipes** for you and your family's enjoyment
- **Recipes that your kids will love**
- And much, much more…

So don't wait, follow this link: https://dl.bookfunnel.com/pdk6lr9rnr, and start cooking the world's most famous food in your own kitchen for free!

A Message from the Author

First of all, thank you for reading this book. I know you could have picked any number of books to read, but you picked this book and for that, I am extremely grateful.

I hope that it adds value and quality to your life.

If you enjoyed this book and found benefit in reading it, I'd love to hear from you and I also hope that you could take some time to post a review on the site where you purchased it from. Your feedback and support will help me to greatly improve my writing craft for future projects and make this book even better.

Thank you,
Michael Marino

Made in the USA
Coppell, TX
01 April 2022

75890327R00077